BARRON'S B...

THOM...
HARDY'S

# Return of
the Native

BY

Charles Flowers

SERIES EDITOR

Michael Spring
Editor, *Literary Cavalcade*
Scholastic Inc.

BARRON'S EDUCATIONAL SERIES, INC.
Woodbury New York / London / Toronto / Sydney

hours of work
to making the

© Copyright 1984 by Barron's Educational Series, Inc.

*All inquiries should be addressed to:*
Barron's Educational Series, Inc.
113 Crossways Park Drive
Woodbury, New York 11797

*Library of Congress Catalog Card No. 84-18440*

International Standard Book No. 0-8120-3439-2

**Library of Congress Cataloging in Publication Data**
Flowers, Charles.
  Thomas Hardy's Return of the native.

  (Barron's book notes)
  Bibliography: p. 118
  Summary: A guide to reading "Return of the Native" with
a critical and appreciative mind. Includes background on
the author's life and times, sample tests, term paper
suggestions, and a reading list.
  1. Hardy, Thomas,  1840–1928. Return of the native.
[1. Hardy, Thomas, 1840—1928. Return of the native.
2. English literature—History and criticism] I. Title
II. Series.
PR4747.F59   1984      823'.8      84-18440
ISBN 0-8120-3439-2 (pbk.)

PRINTED IN THE UNITED STATES OF AMERICA

456      550      987654321

# CONTENTS

iv

# ADVISORY BOARD

We wish to thank the following educators who helped us focus our *Book Notes* series to meet student needs and critiqued our manuscripts to provide quality materials.

# HOW TO USE THIS BOOK

You have to know how to approach literature in order to get the most out of it. This *Barron's Book Notes* volume follows a plan based on methods used by some of the best students to read a work of literature.

Begin with the guide's section on the author's life and times. As you read, try to form a clear picture of the author's personality, circumstances, and motives for writing the work. This background usually will make it easier for you to hear the author's tone of voice, and follow where the author is heading.

Then go over the rest of the introductory material—such sections as those on the plot, characters, setting, themes, and style of the work. Underline, or write down in your notebook, particular things to watch for, such as contrasts between characters and repeated literary devices. At this point, you may want to develop a system of symbols to use in marking your text as you read. (Of course, you should only mark up a book you own, not one that belongs to another person or a school.) Perhaps you will want to use a different letter for each character's name, a different number for each major theme of the book, a different color for each important symbol or literary device. Be prepared to mark up the pages of your book as you read. Put your marks in the margins so you can find them again easily.

Now comes the moment you've been waiting for—the time to start reading the work of literature. You may want to put aside your *Barron's Book Notes* volume until you've read the work all the way through. Or you may want to alternate, reading the *Book Notes* analysis of each section as soon as you have finished reading the corresponding part of the original. Before you move on, reread crucial passages you don't fully understand. (Don't take this guide's analysis for granted—make up your own mind as to what the work means.)

Once you've finished the whole work of literature, you may want to review it right away, so you can firm up your ideas about what it means. You may want to leaf through the book concentrating on passages you marked in reference to one character or one theme. This is also a good time to reread the *Book Notes* introductory material, which pulls together insights on specific topics.

When it comes time to prepare for a test or to write a paper, you'll already have formed ideas about the work. You'll be able to go back through it, refreshing your memory as to the author's exact words and perspective, so that you can support your opinions with evidence drawn straight from the work. Patterns will emerge, and ideas will fall into place; your essay question or term paper will almost write itself. Give yourself a dry run with one of the sample tests in the guide. These tests present both multiple-choice and essay questions. An accompanying section gives answers to the multiple-choice questions as well as suggestions for writing the essays. If you have to select a term paper topic, you may choose one from the list of suggestions in this book. This guide also provides you with a reading list, to help you when you start research for a term paper, and a selection of provocative comments by critics, to spark your thinking before you write.

# THE AUTHOR
# AND HIS TIMES

Today's readers may find Thomas Hardy's outlook
stern and grim. Hardy, however, was beloved in his
own time. In an age when the Industrial Revolution
was bringing dramatic and sometimes disturbing
change to England, he celebrated the nation's roots in
its rural past. In an age when new ideas like Darwin's
theory of evolution challenged traditional religious
beliefs, Hardy showed that even the simplest people
have always wrestled with similar timeless questions:
How are we to live? What determines our fate? Are
we really independent beings? He spoke directly to
the concerns of people trembling on the brink of a
new era.

Though he dealt with serious questions, Hardy was
an immensely popular novelist because he believed in
telling a good story. And he liked to write about ordinary people. Their problems, their triumphs or de-
feats, were in his view the most important material for
any novelist.

Born in 1840, Hardy grew up in middle-class comfort near the provincial English town of Dorchester.
His father was a stone mason, successful enough that
he could afford to employ assistants. His mother, who
wanted a better class of life, made certain that her son
was educated in the classics. Young Hardy showed a
gift for language early, but when it came time to
choose a career, he went off to become an architect,
spending some years in London. As he worked at that
trade, however, his literary talent inevitably asserted
itself. He started to publish fiction; he began to get

recognition for it. Eventually, after marrying Emma
Gifford, a church organist from London, he returned
to the Wessex countryside, the scene of *The Return of
the Native*. Until his death at 87, he remained in the
area, writing novels and, later, poetry, living simply
and quietly despite world-wide fame.

His writing, however, reveals a mind and a soul
that are anything but quiet. He questions the conven-
tions of his day—marriage, for instance. He probes
into the complexities of human psychology, of religion, of political theory. Though he lived in isolation,
he was in touch with all the intellectual upheavals of
the age. And it was an exciting, puzzling time. The
recent invention of the steam engine had made travel
fast and easy, and people suddenly had a different
perception of distance, even of time. Suddenly, facto-
ries were springing up everywhere, and the quick
money offered by new industries drew people from
the farmlands to city slums. Typical English life,
which had been rural, now took on a new character.
People began to see themselves and their fellow men
in a different light. The British government responded
to these social changes by passing laws to guarantee
conditions we take for granted today: voting rights for
all social classes; regulations to promote health and
sanitation; and programs to help the poor, the ill, and
the elderly. Many of the ideas in the air could fairly be
called "liberal," and they probably have much to do
with Clym Yeobright's ideas in *The Return of the
Native*.

The nineteenth century also faced Darwin's shocking (or exciting, depending on one's point of view)
theory of evolution. The Bible seemed to be brought
into question, as Darwin suggested that man had
evolved from a lower animal rather than being created
by God in God's own image. Organized religion stag-

gered from this blow. And evolutionary theory was just one of many scientific discoveries that were changing the way people thought about the nature of existence. Hardy was well aware of these intellectual trends. Though he wrote about uneducated rural characters in lonely hamlets, he wrote from the point of view of a thinker who questions traditional beliefs. This voice is, clearly, that of an agnostic. He does not know whether or not God exists; he does not know if the universe works upon principles of justice.

Grim as his philosophical views may be, Hardy delights us with his lively individuals and his love of the English countryside. Like Shakespeare, he has a fine ear for local dialects. He had a painter's eye for dramatic scenes in nature. His heart goes out to the enduring decency of simple country people who work hard and do not indulge themselves in idleness or selfishness.

Is he too hard on characters like Eustacia Vye, who yearns for the city life Hardy spurned, or on Damon Wildeve, who cares for little but money and pleasure? Perhaps. Hardy often seems to be a stern and rigorous moralist. To balance this, however, he finds some hope in the homely virtues of characters like Thomasin Yeobright or Diggory Venn.

Though Hardy isn't exactly a cheerful writer, his novels are hard to put down. The reader is gripped by a sense of life rushing irrevocably onward. We become involved in the characters' dilemmas, and with them we feel torn between what people think they want and what life actually brings them in the end.

Unquestionably, Hardy speaks directly and powerfully to some need within us all. We, too, question fate. We, too, hope that unselfishness will be rewarded. *The Return of the Native*, condemned by critics when it first appeared, may be Hardy's greatest novel. It has faults, many of which may strike you right away. But the story and its unforgettable characters will lodge in your consciousness. You may find yourself thinking, "Yes, this is how life is." You may even begin to see the eternal questions which Hardy ponders cropping up in your own daily life. You are about to read a tale of country life, but it is really a story of the greater world in which human beings have always lived, and will forever live.

# THE NOVEL

## The Plot

In a neglected, wild area of the English countryside, bonfires are being lit to mark the coming of winter. As the countryfolk celebrate this ancient custom, we learn that the emotional lives of several people are in turmoil. Thomasin Yeobright, niece of the highly respectable Mrs. Yeobright, has been stood up on her wedding day. Disgraced, she has returned home. Wildeve, the man she was engaged to, (against her aunt's wishes), is a handsome lady-killer who has failed as an engineer and now runs an inn and tavern named The Quiet Woman. He still pledges to marry Thomasin, but secretly he is torn between her and Eustacia Vye, a strange and beautiful young woman who lives with her grandfather, a retired sea captain. The Vyes' lonely cottage is situated in the middle of Egdon Heath, a great wasteland that is the center of the novel's action.

For some weeks, Wildeve cannot make up his mind. Thomasin, for the sake of appearances, wants to marry him, even though she is now well aware of his weakness. Eustacia, who has been passionately attracted to him for a year, sees him as the only pleasure in her dull life in a part of the country she hates. A curious character, Diggory Venn, hangs around watching developments. He once proposed to Thomasin and was turned down, but he still hopes that she may give him another chance. Because Thomasin rejected him, he gave up a comfortable life on a dairy farm and has taken up the trade of reddlemaking.

This occupation dyes his skin red, making him a social outcast.

As Christmas nears, word comes that Mrs. Yeobright's son, Clym, is returning from Paris for a visit. Eustacia has never met him, but the tales of his success in the diamond business arouse her interest. Here may be the heroic figure she's been waiting for all her life. He becomes a glamorous fantasy for her. To meet him, she disguises herself as a boy and performs in a Christmas play at his mother's house. They meet and find each other fascinating, although he does not yet learn her true identity.

Caring only for Thomasin's happiness, Diggory asks Eustacia to give up her hold on Wildeve. Since Clym has arrived, she is bored with Wildeve, so she writes him a rejection letter. Stunned, he immediately asks Thomasin once again to marry him. He gets her consent moments before Diggory arrives at her door, hoping to propose to her himself.

Eustacia disguises herself and appears at the wedding. When she is asked, as a "stranger," to act as an official witness, she triumphantly shows her face to Wildeve. He thought his marriage would hurt her, despite what she had written to him. It is, however, just what she wants to happen—at the moment.

Soon, Clym and Eustacia begin meeting each other on the heath. The countryside is coming into flower, and their love begins to blossom. Worried, Mrs. Yeobright warns her son against Eustacia as an idle creature. Clym is already in love, however, and mother and son quarrel bitterly. Eventually, he leaves her house for good, setting up in a small cottage six miles away. After a passionate nighttime encounter, Eustacia and Clym decide to marry immediately. He plans to remain in the Egdon area and become a schoolmaster, a decision that disturbs both Mrs. Yeobright and Eustacia. The young woman is convinced, however, that he will soon change his mind. She dreams of nothing more than escape to the excitement of Clym's Parisian life.

On the night of their wedding there is a terrible misunderstanding. Mrs. Yeobright hopes to be reconciled with her son by sending a wedding gift, his share of the inheritance from his father. An equal amount of money is due Thomasin. Christian Cantle, a simple-minded fellow, is supposed to take both sums to the wedding party. On the way, however, he stops by The Quiet Woman where he wins a raffle. His luck makes him think that fortune is on his side. Soon after, he loses all the Yeobrights' money by playing dice with Wildeve. Diggory immediately appears and wins the money back. Believing the whole sum is Thomasin's, he gives it to her without explanation.

Mrs. Yeobright decides, on the basis of Christian's version of these events, that Wildeve must still have both Clym and Thomasin's shares of the money. She suspects he has given Clym's share to Eustacia. She asks her daughter-in-law, who angrily decides that Mrs. Yeobright is implying an improper relationship between Eustacia and Wildeve. An argument cuts off all hope of friendship between the two headstrong women.

Almost immediately, Eustacia and Clym's marriage begins to founder. He has been studying too hard for his new occupation and develops eye trouble. He is reduced to making a living by gathering wood on the heath, just like one of the country folk. Eustacia becomes depressed, realizing that she has made a horrible mistake and may never escape Egdon. The conflict with his mother preys upon Clym's mind.

To cheer herself up, Eustacia goes off alone to a night of dancing in a nearby village. There, she and Wildeve meet accidentally and dance with abandon. They recall their former passion longingly. Diggory, who sees them together, worries that the affair may be starting again. When Wildeve begins to walk by the Yeobrights' cottage every night, Diggory harasses him from the darkness. Wildeve decides that it is safer to visit Eustacia by daylight.

On an incredibly hot summer day, Mrs. Yeobright decides to walk over to her son's cottage to try to make peace. Just before she arrives, Clym comes in from the fields and falls asleep, exhausted. Wildeve shows up to see Eustacia. When Mrs. Yeobright knocks on the door, Eustacia flees with Wildeve to the garden, thinking that Clym will awaken and let his mother in. In fact, Clym is fast asleep and the door is never opened. But Mrs. Yeobright has seen Eustacia's face at a window and assumes that Clym and his wife have purposely refused to let her in. Fatigued and angered, she starts back homeward.

As Mrs. Yeobright struggles in the afternoon heat, a little boy, Johnny Nunsuch, comes upon her; she tells him that she has been abandoned by her son. That night, Clym decides to go to his mother and ask for-giveness. On the way, he finds her collapsed and unconscious on the heath. He carries her to shelter and calls the villagers for help. She has been bitten by a snake, but when the doctor arrives, he says that it is exertion that is the real trouble. Mrs. Yeobright dies. Johnny relates what the woman told him about her son abandoning her, and Clym decides that he is guilty of his mother's death.

After weeks of delirium, Clym finally calms down. Eustacia is miserable, sure that her role in Mrs. Yeo-bright's death will be discovered, but she says nothing. By chance, Clym learns from Diggory that his mother had intended to visit the day she died. He asks Johnny for more information and learns that Mrs. Yeobright had indeed knocked on the door but was turned away. He also learns that Eustacia was in the house with an unidentified man.

Furious, Clym accuses Eustacia of killing his mother. He wants to know what happened and the name of the man. Eustacia refuses to talk. After a wild argument, she leaves Clym. He is distraught but he cannot forgive her. Ironically, Thomasin has just had Wildeve's baby and named her Eustacia Clementine, after her cousin and his wife.

Back at her grandfather's cottage, Eustacia contemplates suicide. Charley, the hired boy, who idolizes her, prevents her from doing so. Soon, Wildeve visits. He has inherited a large sum of money and can now travel the world. He offers to help her, hoping she will become his mistress and leave Egdon with him. Eustacia cannot make up her mind.

Partly under Thomasin's influence, Clym decides to tell Eustacia that he wants her back. He writes a letter but waits before sending it. Meanwhile, Eustacia signals Wildeve that she will leave with him at midnight. Clym's letter finally arrives, but it is not delivered to her, since she has pretended to go to bed. As a terrible storm begins to savage the heath, she slips out of the house to meet Wildeve. On the way, however, she realizes that escape with him is no solution. Losing all hope, she begins to wander away.

Meanwhile, her grandfather has gone searching for her and goes to alert Clym. Thomasin is also out in the storm, with her baby, urging Clym to prevent Wildeve from eloping with Eustacia. In the raging storm, Clym does indeed meet up with Wildeve, just as the sound of a body falling into a pond is heard. The two men rush over to try to save Eustacia from a swirling whirlpool. Diggory comes upon the struggle at the pond; he dives in and pulls out the unconscious bodies of Clym and Wildeve. With help that arrives, he finds Eustacia, too. Clym recovers, but the former lovers are dead. Clym now thinks himself guilty of the deaths of two women.

A year and a half after the tragedy, Diggory has given up reddlemaking and become a dairy farmer. At a Maypole celebration, he pretends to be in love with an unknown girl who has lost a glove. When Thomasin discovers that the glove is hers, she realizes that she now loves Diggory. They are married, as the villagers celebrate. Clym, who has renewed his studies, becomes a traveling preacher. His message is that we should all love one another. He is respected for his ideas and also for the sorrows that he has endured.

# The Characters

## Eustacia Vye

Is Eustacia really a superior being, or does she merely think she is? Are her passions deeper than other people's, or is she simply greedy? Is she doomed by fate or by her own selfishness? Few readers have ever been able to decide for certain. That is the genius of Hardy's portrayal. If you are like most readers, you will find this beautiful young woman fascinating one moment, exasperating the next. Even the other characters of the novel find her unpredictable, and their reactions to her vary widely. Is she a goddess or a witch?

Hardy skillfully avoids simple answers by showing us many sides of this complex character. At times, he seems sympathetic to her frustrations with her narrow life, yet he does not shrink from showing her at her worst. She is capable of deception, and she has a killing temper. She can be disloyal, she can wound with a perfectly aimed insult, and she can exploit other people's good nature.

Why, then, does the reader simply not turn away from her? Perhaps because almost everyone can feel pity for her at moments, such as before her death when she cries out, "How I have tried and tried to be a splendid woman, and how destiny has been against me! . . . I do not deserve my lot!" If she had been able to live in a great city, perhaps she would have been splendid. If she had found a society that appreciated her rare qualities, rather than fearing or scorning them as the people of Egdon do, she might have achieved great things.

Hardy's point, of course, is that those possibilities are not available. Like all of us, Eustacia must make do with the situation that faces her: she must either accept or change her fate. Her tragedy is that she refuses to accept it but fails to change it.

Usually, Hardy describes Eustacia in contrasts, to stress the divided nature of her soul, the conflicts that torture her. Early in the novel, he writes, "As far as social ethics were concerned Eustacia approached the savage state, though in emotion she was all the while an epicure. She had advanced to the secret recesses of sensuousness, yet had hardly crossed the threshold of conventionality." He is saying that, on the positive side she is a nonconformist, an independent spirit; but on the negative side, emotion, passion, the heart's needs have become an obsession with her. She lives solely for romance. "To be loved to madness—such was her great desire."

One side of her nature, however, all too poignantly recognizes that love itself is evanescent: she is terrified of time. Think of her first appearance in the novel, eagerly searching with her telescope for Damon. She is the very picture of a desperate woman searching for experience. She carries with her an hourglass, even though, as Hardy takes pains to point out, she does have a modern watch. It is as if she actually wants to see time, her dreaded enemy, as it dribbles away. At the moment which should be her most blissful, when she and Clym decide to marry, she gazes toward the eclipsed moon and warns, "See how our time is slipping, slipping, slipping!" She confides to her lover the deep (and perceptive) fear that their love will not last.

Though she lives by certain illusions, another side of Eustacia is ruthlessly realistic. Perhaps her most attractive quality is this inability to lie to herself about herself. Basically, she knows her own faults; she's intelligent, perceptive, and honest. When she first meets Clym, she explains to him that she is depressed by life. It's a simple statement, but it may well sum up all her difficulties. Life itself is somehow too much for her unusually sensitive and demanding nature. Life doesn't give her what she wants. Life, as she experiences it, is a prison.

Not surprisingly, readers disagree on many aspects of this puzzling, ambiguous character. Her actions can be seen from many different perspectives. For example, some say that she sincerely loves Clym; yet surely she also has a selfish motive in agreeing to marry him: in her mind, the marriage is associated with an escape to Paris. Throughout the book, her mixed motives often lead to troubling actions.

No matter how many times you read this novel, you will probably never be certain just how you feel about Eustacia Vye. She is too contradictory; she is too special and rare. Hardy himself is most eloquent when he describes her in symbolic terms, as when he writes that she and Damon, walking together under the full moon, "appeared amid the expanse like two pearls on a table of ebony." Equally doomed, these two passionate beings shine brightly in a dark world only to be extinguished.

## Damon Wildeve

Romantic Wildeve is a striking contrast to Hardy's plain, honest country folk. His past is shady. He has failed at his career as an engineer, perhaps because of laziness; he seems never to have failed with women, however. More than anyone else in the novel, he cares about money and is usually strangely lucky in getting it. This man has never had to work hard for anything.

Thoughtless, handsome, eager for what he cannot have, Damon Wildeve is not a strong or a likeable character. He seems to have no friends and no family connections, although he is sexually irresistible to many young women. He seems unusually sophisticated for the wilds of Egdon—much like Eustacia. The crucial difference between them is his overriding weakness. He does not have her high standards or her depth of feeling. In fact, Hardy often shows Wildeve taking rash steps almost frivolously, like someone gambling with life. He just can't take other people's needs too seriously. He isn't evil, but he is so self-centered that other people suffer.

What Wildeve wants most is comfort and pleasure, a life of ease. Even Eustacia, who partly shares these desires, knows that he is really not very substantial;

she's quickly diverted from him when Clym arrives, and only returns to Wildeve when Clym disappoints her. When Wildeve dies, he is not mourned long. His only legacy, a daughter, is ironically the product of a marriage to Thomasin that he really wanted to avoid.

Yet perhaps we can feel sorry for Wildeve, caught up in the tragic web of circumstances, too weak to resist the fate that sweeps him along. Is Wildeve a villain—a liar, gambler, and seducer? Or is he simply a shallow man who has blundered into a more tumultuous world than he was meant for? Consider both possibilities as you read the novel.

## Thomasin Yeobright

Countrified and inexperienced, Thomasin seems to be less complex and interesting than the other major characters. So far as we can tell, she is not as passionate as Eustacia, as intellectually profound as Clym, as sophisticated as Wildeve, or as intuitively insightful as Mrs. Yeobright. Hardy likens her to a bird, and she often flits through a scene, scattering good cheer but not pausing to alight. And yet, it is Thomasin who gets (and perhaps deserves, in Hardy's view) a happy life, in conventional terms. As the novel comes to a close, Thomasin feels fulfilled, as a loving mother and beloved wife. The more ambitious characters have exposed themselves too openly to fate; she is content with her lot, rooted to the heath where she has grown up, comfortable with the simple life of the Egdon area. She belongs. There is no conflict between what she is and where she is.

Perhaps, in that sense, she is the most fortunate character in the novel. Unhappiness does come to her, but only when some element intrudes that rubs against the grain of ordinary Egdon life—Wildeve's attraction, Eustacia's rivalry, even Clym's return from Paris. Although she is drawn to Wildeve, he does not belong on Egdon Heath, and ultimately she cannot be happy with someone who is so foreign to (and contemptuous of) the ideas, people, and land that her life is tied to. Diggory, on the other hand—who actually lives on the open heath—is a good match for her.

Uncomplicated as she may be, however, Thomasin is no fool. She marries Wildeve with her eyes open; she has a pretty good idea of his faults. Without being told or shown, she recognizes when his passion for Eustacia comes back to life. Eventually, when she is free, she comes to appreciate Diggory's deep, slow, and silent commitment to her.

Perhaps more important than what she sees, however, is what she wants to see. For example, when Clym and his mother are not speaking, she tries to act the role of peacemaker. When Clym is estranged from Eustacia, again Thomasin urges reconciliation. She does not like conflict. Perhaps Hardy, who doesn't support traditional Christian ideas in this novel, nonetheless believes somewhat in the New Testament idea, "Blessed are the peacemakers." Thomasin is good because she is concerned for the good of others. She is in harmony with her world; she wants to share that harmony.

Alone among the major characters, Thomasin represents the continuity of human life. Clym cannot bring himself to marry again, but she can. Motherhood is important to her; she won't even let the hired nurse carry her child. Why is she finally attracted to Diggory? He is a dairy farmer and has been a reddleman—in both cases, working with the basics of sustaining life. These two are meant for each other; for example, on the stormy night when Wildeve and Eustacia drown, Thomasin lets Diggory carry her child. She shows no one else this basic form of trust.

Oddly, Thomasin has little personal history on the page before us—no parents, no siblings, no close personal friends. Who is she? Who or what has influenced her most? In some ways, she resembles Mrs. Yeobright; also, she is clearly affected by Clym's opinions. Finally, though, it may be best to see her, as Hardy does, as a birdlike creature who finds Egdon Heath her native habitat. She flourishes there. To understand her, we would have to understand the mysterious heath itself.

## Clym Yeobright

Well-meaning, intelligent in certain ways, Clym Yeobright is not suited to life in the real world of his day. He dislikes city life as "effeminate," but when he returns to Egdon, no one understands his ambition to teach school. His ideas come from books rather than from direct experience with people. Unfortunately, he does not really know himself, either. He thinks he is rational and controlled; but love for Eustacia causes him to act rashly. He thinks he is morally right; but this leads him to be cruel to others, whom he believes to be in the wrong.

Like his cousin Thomasin, Clym loves Egdon Heath, and the people there love him for his pure nature. The most important influence in his life is his home, especially his mother, Mrs. Yeobright. Temporarily, he leaves her to marry Eustacia, but in the end, even after her death, her influence on him remains strong.

Hardy suggests that Clym is too sensitive. His constant thinking almost seems to weaken him physically; his studying literally makes him an invalid for a while. His high ideas are not very practical. In day-to-day experiences with other people, he often has little or no idea what they want, or what they are thinking. Yet this does not make him ridiculous. We have to respect him because he is struggling to find the truth of life. Though he is sometimes obtuse, he is never thoughtless. Perhaps he lacks the sense of self that is necessary to survive. If Wildeve is too selfish, then Clym in contrast is too unselfish.

In the end, Clym dedicates himself to others, hoping to spread truth and comfort and to teach all men to love each other. Ironically, he himself has failed with his mother and with Eustacia, the two people he loved most. He is more successful at loving all mankind than at being a son or husband.

## Mrs. Yeobright

Clym's mother has definite limitations. She is snobbish, even though her own social position would not be very high outside Egdon. She is stubborn and likes to get her own way; she interferes, with disastrous consequences. On the other hand, her judgments about people turn out to be remarkably accurate. Also, her deep love for Clym and for Thomasin always wins out over her temper, and she is willing to forgive. She has a strong sense of fairness; for example, she does her best to be polite to Wildeve.

Like her son and niece, Mrs. Yeobright feels at home in Egdon. Her life there is simple and unpretentious, in tune with the community. She is part of an older generation, so perhaps we can forgive her for trying to manipulate the young people. What chiefly

motivates her is love for Clym. She wants him to be
successful financially, married to someone who will
be devoted to him. And yet, without knowing it con-
sciously, she also probably wants to keep him for herself.

In addition to being a strong central character, Mrs.
Yeobright is also a kind of symbol. She is the last rep-
resentative of her generation. Even at Egdon, change
is on the way. For Hardy, she may well embody both
the faults and virtues of a particular time and place
that's rapidly passing away.

## Diggory Venn

Strong and silent, Diggory Venn is not what he
seems to be. At night, he looks like a demon, but he
has the morals of an angel. People think he is low on
the social scale, but he can at any time return to being
a successful farmer. He is also "artful," able to disguise his true feelings, when he is courting the one
love of his life, Thomasin.

Diggory is, of course, almost too good to be true. To
many readers, he almost appears to be a supernatural
being. He arrives in the nick of time, when ever
Thomasin seems to be in danger. He can move swiftly
across the heath at night; he can beat the lucky gambler Wildeve, even with Wildeve's own dice. It seems
Diggory can almost read men's minds. Capable, insightful, loyal, he performs the role of a guardian
angel.

It is easy to see why Hardy originally thought that
Diggory should simply disappear at the end of the
novel, instead of settling down with Thomasin. Diggory is too fantastic a creation to fit easily into an ordinary homelife. However, he says he has entered this

strange life as a reddleman only because Thomasin rejected him; to marry her, then, he returns to normal society.

Though his actions seem magical, Diggory's heart is totally human. It is part of his appeal that Diggory steadfastly loves Thomasin. She is not clever or sophisticated, and she has been foolish. She is generous, however, and her heart is in the right place. Diggory unlike Clym and Wildeve, falls in love for reasons that may cause love to last. He combines Clym's sense of justice with a practical understanding of how men and women actually live their lives.

# Other Elements

## SETTING

Huge, forbidding, strange—the wasteland of Egdon Heath is like a stage set for the action of this novel. It offers wide spaces for movement, but it also has hiding-places for intimate scenes. Its many different faces reflect or heighten the many different moods of the story. One can believe that the Heath has many secrets, and has witnessed all possible varieties of human experience. It is a place of long life and of sudden death, of fertile spring and short, vivid summer. No matter what feeling Hardy wants to express at any particular point, the heath can offer it up.

Something about Egdon Heath depresses the restless, adventure-seeking characters of the novel, Eustacia and Wildeve. But it is a comforting presence to unselfish people like Clym and Thomasin. As you read, notice each character's reaction to the heath; it may say something about his or her inner nature. The less intellectual country folk simply take the place for granted, just as they take their own souls for granted.

Does Egdon Heath represent life? Time? The supernatural? Destiny? Readers have suggested these and other possibilities. Perhaps it is not a symbol for anything, but merely a background, a small universe, having no meaning, offering no answers. Part of the mysterious appeal of this novel is that Hardy makes the heath seem so significant, but then never specifically explains his purposes. We must use our own imaginations to try to understand and feel what the heath finally means.

## THEMES

### 1. THE UNHAPPINESS OF ALL HUMAN LIFE

The only sustained happiness in the novel may come at the end, in Thomasin's and Diggory's marriage, and Hardy had originally planned a less happy ending even for them. The lives of the other major characters all end in tragic death, like Eustacia and Wildeve, or continue in sadness like Clym. There are moments of ecstasy, from time to time, but they pass quickly away. Hardy's message seems to be that people cannot expect to experience joy; they are fortunate if they can at least avoid great pain.

### 2. THE POWER OF FATE OVER HUMAN INTENT

Often, characters, in the novel try to control the future. They try to arrange for their own happiness and for that of others. Just as often, fate comes between a character and his or her best-laid plans. Is

Hardy saying that fate is ruled by evil intent? No. In this novel, fate seems simply not to care about human beings. It intervenes just as often to thwart well-meaning plans as to upset wicked ones. Fate is more powerful than the desires of individuals.

### 3. A STUDY OF VANISHING RURAL LIFE

Egdon's colorful dialect, seasonal celebrations, superstitious folk beliefs—these were disappearing even as Hardy wrote the novel. He loved his native countryside and tried to re-create both the land and the people. But he is a faithful historian, and so he shows the bad with the good. He is not blind to the faults of uneducated, unsophisticated country folk, he knows they can be cruelly prejudiced, as well as loyal. They can be foolishly ignorant, as well as dependable. Like Clym, though, Hardy clearly prefers life in the country to life in the cities. In spite of his realistic portrayals, a nostalgia colors the rustic scenes, for Hardy is sorry to see the changes that progress will bring to the villages of his youth.

### 4. THE GREATNESS OF UNKNOWN PEOPLE

Hardy's main characters are not much in the eyes of the world: an innkeeper, a curate's daughter, a self-taught traveling preacher, a dissatisfied young girl. He believes, however, that obscure people have lives just as important and troubling as the lives of famous people; that's why he brings in references to classical and historical figures, to add a heroic dimension to the lives of these ordinary people. They feel as deeply as great heroes do; their mistakes are as tragic; their deaths are no less (and no more) significant. Writers in other periods had written about great kings or mythical heroes. Hardy wanted to portray the intensity of life among ordinary people.

## 5. PASSION

For Hardy, romantic passion can be dangerous. Another kind of passion, uncontrolled anger, can also have unfortunate consequences. The only feelings which can be trusted are moderate, like Thomasin's kindness and desire for people to be at peace with each other. Relationships between people are best not when they are violent and sudden, but when they have a long history and have endured much, like the love between Diggory and Thomasin. Love at first sight, as Eustacia and Clym find out, is likely to be a mistake. Hot-tempered reactions are generally a mistake, as well. Hardy understands that passion is fundamental to human nature—and he portrays passion so well that we cannot help but respond to it in characters like Eustacia. But he stresses that we must try to act in the light of reason. We may fail—as Clym does—but we must try. Moderation is the goal.

## 6. A PORTRAIT OF CLYM

Well meaning if sometimes mistaken, Clym is Hardy's central character, the returning native of the novel's title. He does not find happiness, but he does find a kind of wisdom through his suffering. In the beginning, he is stubborn and proud. When he discovers that he can cause tragedy for others, he learns humility. Hardy wants the reader to learn what Clym learns. We cannot always get what we want in life, but neither can anyone else. Human beings should love one another and try not to cause each other pain.

## 7. THE UNCHANGING NATURE OF HUMAN EXISTENCE

Often, Hardy pulls back from his story to talk about the past. He refers frequently to famous characters in classical myths, the Bible, or history, perhaps to show that people in all civilizations have had much the same problems and have probably had the same questions about existence. Ancient peoples have been forgotten, and so will we. Egdon Heath is a symbol of this timelessness; throughout its seasons and cycles, it remains essentially the same. There are storms, and there are bright summer days, but the true nature of the heath never really alters. Human life, too, has its storms and bright days, but its essential nature never changes, either.

## 8. THE ROLE OF NATURE

For Hardy, nature could have many moods. He uses natural descriptions in several ways: to reflect a character's inner emotions, to symbolize the conflicts of human life, to show the comparative insignificance of human beings. Sometimes nature seems to help mankind; sometimes nature seems to turn against us. It is as mysterious as fate. In this novel, Hardy investigates these and other aspects of nature; but he also takes obvious delight in describing various kinds of natural beauty for their own sake. Anyone with unusual skill likes to exercise that skill, and Hardy enjoys writing his famous descriptions: the romantic loveliness and excitement of the heath by moonlight, the burning heat of the afternoon Mrs. Yeobright dies, or the terror of the storm the night of Eustacia's death. Some characters, like Thomasin, are in harmony with this beauty; others, like Eustacia, struggle against it. By making it a powerful presence in this novel, Hardy shows us that nature is a force to be reckoned with.

## 9. THE ROLE OF CHANCE

Is chance the same thing as fate? Different readers disagree on this question. Perhaps it is cruel, deliberate fate that Eustacia, for instance, has been set down to live on the heath she loathes. It may be mere capricious chance, however, that Mrs. Yeobright decides to visit on the very afternoon that Wildeve also decides to come to Eustacia's cottage. In other words, fate seems to rule events according to some vast pattern which is beyond human control. Chance seems to intervene in smaller, random ways, when human beings are trying to act on their own. Many readers, however, feel that chance and fate are the same thing in this novel. Things "just happen," without rhyme or reason, and that in itself is the pattern of the universe.

## STYLE

This novel, written early in his long career, shows Hardy trying out different writing styles. He is always ambitious, but he is not always successful. Occasionally, his poetic descriptions are pretentious and long winded; they become top heavy. In other passages, he tries to record the earthy folk dialect of the Egdon area, and sometimes his attempts to be accurate can become awkward; the dialect gets in the way.

But the achievements of his style far outweigh the few failures. His best descriptions are not simple pictures; they're dramas of life. His most believable conversations have the force, the contradiction, the illogic of actual conversations. He has also created a successful voice in which he can speak directly to the reader. Sometimes it sounds a little formal, but generally it is a useful way to guide us along, as he moves easily from discussions of philosophy, for example, to a portrayal of a simple country scene.

Does Hardy's writing move slowly? Perhaps it does, for us today, conditioned as we are by thirty-second television commercials and three-minute pop songs. In Hardy's own day, however, readers expected to spend long hours every evening in reading a novel, taking plenty of time to think about what was happening. When a novel was published serially, in a magazine, as Hardy's novels first appeared, the experience of reading a novel might go on for months. The pace of Hardy's long, complex sentences is a reflection of the pace of the times.

You can look one by one at the elements of Hardy's prose—the use of dialect vocabulary, the vigorous verbs, the careful explanations—and still not find the secret of his best work. Many readers will recall a favorite scene as brilliantly written. But when they return to the book, the actual words used may not live up to the impression they made. Hardy's gift is to summon up powerful images that take on a life of their own, quite beyond style.

## POINT OF VIEW

Hardy frequently interrupts his story to tell us what it means—but does he really tell us? One can not always be certain that this author is explaining himself fully, even when he seems to be doing so. It's not that he attempts to deceive the reader; rather, he wants to make it clear that life is unclear. He wants to emphasize the mystery of existence. He doesn't believe that life offers simple, clear-cut answers, nor does he imagine that human beings, or his characters, can be judged as either completely good or completely bad.

His point of view, then, could rightly be called "ambiguous." He may directly criticize Wildeve in one passage, for example, but then his narrative suggests that Wildeve is not responsible for everything that happens to him and Eustacia. He may number all of Eustacia's worst faults, but somehow most readers still feel that Hardy is, like Clym, fascinated with her.

He shows that life is filled with disasters and tragedies, but he says that new life will continually spring up to replace the old.

Although Hardy frequently shows a sense of humor, many readers have felt that he puts too much emphasis on the unhappy aspects of life. He would argue against that charge, saying that he simply reported life as it is, and the true report just happens to be filled with unhappiness. Is that the thinking of an objective observer, or a pessimist? As you read this novel, form your own opinion of where Hardy really stands.

## FORM AND STRUCTURE

*The Return of the Native* looks at first like a typical nineteenth-century novel: long, with several plots, and set in a wide landscape. But this tale is really very compact. The major action takes place in a year's time. All of the characters live in the Egdon area, and the outside world does not intrude (we do not hear, for example, about the national problems of England).

All of the major characters are bound together in a dense knot of relationships. The structure of this book is concentrated, to reflect the tight organization of the action. Book First, the longest book, sets the stage and introduces the characters. Book Second brings Clym and Eustacia together and sees the marriage of Thomasin and Wildeve. Book Third shows the split between Clym and his mother and his marriage to Eustacia. Book Fourth tells of the terrible accidents that lead to Mrs. Yeobright's death. Book Fifth sees Clym and Eustacia separate, bringing about the tragic deaths that end the main action. Book Sixth, a kind of epilogue, shows the marriage of Thomasin and Diggory.

The action is organized around seasonal celebrations, beginning and ending with the autumn bonfires, as if to emphasize the dramatic changes that can take place in such short periods of time. The story is told in straight chronological order, without the use of flashbacks or other devices. (This may underscore the story's sense of the straightforward, irresistible movement of time itself.) Regularly, our concentration upon the major characters is broken by the appearance of the country folk, as if for comic relief, to stress the need for the reader to step back and consider the meaning of the tale.

# The Story

As you read this novel, notice Hardy's book and chapter headings. Like many novelists of his time, he used these titles to give insights into his story. He divided the tale into six "books," almost like acts in a play. (The last, as we shall see later, was added because readers did not want a completely unhappy ending.)

## BOOK ONE: THE THREE WOMEN

Hardy's women are almost always more interesting and believable than his male characters. This first book introduces us to three of the most famous: the mysterious and beautiful Eustacia Vye, the naïve but strong-willed Thomasin Yeobright, and Mrs. Yeobright, Thomasin's seemingly arrogant and snobbish aunt. Each will come into conflict with the other two, because each is determined to have her own way.

## CHAPTER 1: A FACE ON WHICH TIME MAKES BUT LITTLE IMPRESSION

This brief chapter is a brooding description of Egdon Heath, setting the scene for the tragic events to come. Readers rarely agree on the exact meaning of this first chapter, but don't be concerned. The vagueness is purposeful. You will see that, as the heath appears again and again throughout the novel, you will remember this first chapter and your understanding will grow and change.

In a passage that suggests a lot about his personal point of view, Hardy says that the heath is very much like human beings—"neither ghastly, hateful, nor ugly . . . but, like man, slighted and enduring." Is this a depressing view of mankind? Many people think so. Others, though, believe that calling mankind "slighted and enduring" places the emphasis on human bravery, on the determination to survive.

The chapter ends with Hardy's stress upon the heath's "ancient permanence." Other things have changed over the centuries; it has not. It represents something eternal. Time? Nature? Fate? Hardy doesn't say. Like a movie director, he moves his lens toward the white highway glowing on the heath at dusk, preparing us for the next chapter.

## CHAPTER 2: HUMANITY APPEARS UPON THE SCENE, HAND IN HAND WITH TROUBLE

The action starts in mystery. Here, far from the sea, an old man in a naval uniform trudges along. He meets a man entirely covered in red, driving a cart.

**NOTE: Reddlemen**     Reddlemen went from farm to farm putting identifying red dyemarks on sheep. The red dye usually coated the reddleman's clothes and skin, so children feared the strange-looking, solitary figures. This one, Hardy notes, seems too "promising" for such a life. Another mystery.

Inside the cart, a woman moans. We learn little about these people; for a few pages, Hardy will leave us hanging, almost as if to slow us down to the leisurely pace of life in these Egdon valleys.

In the growing dark, the cart-man sees a form standing on the most prominent rise in the area, a "barrow" or hill. Then, in a flash, the unexplained figure takes flight. All we learn is that it's a woman and that she apparently runs away because a band of people is gathering at the barrow.

Why does she flee? Who is she? What are these people about to do, in the dark of night on a lonely hill? Hardy will begin to give some of these answers in the next few chapters. For now, notice how he is determined to make us think for ourselves, to notice every clue, every hint, every contradiction. By stimulating us to ask questions about the little things, he also gets us in the habit of asking larger questions, those questions about man's fate that probably don't have simple or concrete answers.

**NOTE: Hardy's View of the Individual**     This chapter indicates how Hardy feels about the human spirit. Our imagination, he says, ignores the group that is arriving and clings instead "to that vanished, solitary figure." In other words, it is the independent person, the one who does not become just another member of conventional society, who is most interesting to us. With that in mind, as you read the novel, ask yourself which characters are the most interesting to you personally—those who fit happily into the unchanging life of Egdon, or those who want something different?

---

## CHAPTER 3: THE CUSTOM OF THE COUNTRY

As the chapter title indicates, we are now going to see a typical scene of rural life in the Egdon area early in the nineteenth century

---

**NOTE: Hardy's Rustic Scenes**   Hardy was scarcely born before these customs were dying out, but he had heard about them from older people. Clearly, he delights in recreating them. In fact, all of his scenes with country folk are funny, lively and natural. It may take a few pages for the Egdon dialect to become completely clear to you, but you will pick it up gradually, just as you would the special slang of a new school or city you move to.

---

Before anyone speaks, we see them building a giant bonfire. Other fires are also being lit across the low flat landscape. British readers would know that this is the custom of a particular holiday, November 5, or Guy Fawkes Day, commemorating a plot to blow up Parliament in the early seventeenth century.

**NOTE:  The Bonfire**    The bonfire, like the heath itself, is a symbol of continuity. Springing out of an ancient pagan ritual, it is also a symbol, says Hardy, of "man's rebelliousness" against the coming of winter, almost a defiance of Nature.

---

As the country folk begin to talk and joke, we meet several colorful characters: Grandfer Cantle, an old man who wants only to sing and dance; his son, Christian, who is morbidly fearful and superstitious; Humphrey and Fairway, who are the salt of the earth, honest and unassuming; Olly Dowden, a decent, contented woman. These characters act like the chorus in classical Greek drama; they describe and comment upon the actions of their social superiors. Hardy is also using this bantering, gossipy scene for "exposition," a literary term for giving the background of the story. We learn about a young couple, Thomasin Yeobright and Damon Wildeve, who have just been married. We learn that the bride's aunt, Mrs. Yeobright, had opposed the marriage.

We learn that some folk are disturbed that the pair went to another village to marry and that they haven't been seen since. We also hear that soon Mrs. Yeobright's son Clym, clever and remembered with real affection, will be coming home for a visit. He is the "Native" of the novel's title.

Now that Hardy has laid down the events with which the plot begins, he skillfully brings other major characters briefly "on stage," to introduce us to them. As the bonfire dies down, our attention is drawn to a single bonfire blazing beside the cottage where Captain Vye lives with his granddaughter Eustacia. The villagers' dance is interrupted by the startling appear-

ance of the reddleman. He asks directions to Mrs.
Yeobright's house and leaves, but then the formidable
figure of Mrs. Yeobright herself arrives, to ask gentle
Olly to accompany her to The Quiet Woman inn
where her newly married niece should be waiting by
now.

Before going on to the next chapter, consider how
much information has been packed into this one.
We've met many characters and heard many tales,
but we have also learned something about local feelings (such as the generally lackadaisical attitude toward regular church-going and the wry assumptions
about married life). Some more mysteries have been
raised (for example, why *does* the marriage take place
elsewhere?). Other mysteries seem to have been
solved, for now we know something about Eustacia,
the solitary figure on the barrow, and Captain Vye,
the old man on the road in Chapter 2. It's amazing
that Hardy has achieved so much exposition in a
scene of realistic merrymaking.

## CHAPTER 4: THE HALT ON THE TURNPIKE ROAD

Mrs. Yeobright explains to Olly that she finally
agreed to Thomasin's marriage because she decided
that her niece should "marry where she wished." In
reply to that, Olly, just before taking a separate path,
comments that "her [Thomasin's] feelings got the better of her."

---

**NOTE: Hardy's Distrust of Feelings**    This seemingly casual remark is very important in Hardy's
world. Should feelings be followed? Remember, di-
vorce was inconceivable in this place and time.
Should a lifetime decision be made solely upon the

basis of one's personal desires? As you read, try to figure out Hardy's answer to this question.

---

At this point, there occurs one of those coincidences which disturb some readers of Hardy's novels. (We will see many more of them; consider whether this novelist thinks that human affairs really are determined by pure chance.) Just outside the inn, Mrs. Yeobright runs into the reddleman, who is identified as Diggory Venn. It turns out that Thomasin is the woman asleep in his cart. Now we have met the third of the important "three women." Thomasin's naturally hopeful face is marred by "a film of anxiety and grief." While Diggory is within earshot, Mrs. Yeobright seems calm, if concerned about this peculiar event. When he's gone, however, her sharp question—"Now, Thomasin, what's the meaning of this disgraceful performance?"—reveals just how upset she is.

## CHAPTER 5: PERPLEXITY AMONG HONEST PEOPLE

*Perplexity* means "bewilderment." Honest people are often bewildered because they cannot imagine the motives of devious, tricky people. In this chapter we'll see both honest and devious behavior.

What has happened during Thomasin's wedding day? Even Thomasin, cannot be sure. The parson said there was "some trifling irregularity" in the marriage license, and Thomasin panicked and ran away with Venn, who just happened to be near the church. Did she subconsciously not want the marriage to take place? Did she suspect that Wildeve really didn't want to marry her? We're left to guess. But unlike us, Mrs.

Yeobright can ask questions directly, and characteristically she decides to have it out with Wildeve at once.

Now we meet Wildeve, who is unforgettably described as "one in whom no man would have seen anything to admire, and in whom no woman would have seen anything to dislike." That says it all. Do you need to know his color of eyes, the shape of his head, the color of his hair after that wonderful description? Everybody has known at least one Wildeve.

The scene that follows between Thomasin and Wildeve is strained. The guiltless Thomasin apologizes again and again; the obviously self-centered Wildeve complains that his "sensitiveness" has been hurt by the day's debacle. Nonetheless, he promises to make the marriage good, "carelessly" giving her his hand.

---

**NOTE: Thomasin's Reputation** Why doesn't Thomasin walk out right then? Remember, she went off alone with Wildeve, supposedly to get married. At this point, her reputation is in grave danger. Social rules have changed since then, and we may find it difficult to understand her moral predicament precisely. But we still have some social rules we believe in today. Thomasin is like the people we know who will not, or cannot, break those rules and feel decent.

---

Suddenly, a grotesque thing happens. It might be comic, if it weren't so embarrassing: the townsfolk come, with all good intentions, to serenade the newlyweds. To save *his* reputation, Wildeve pretends the wedding went off smoothly. To Thomasin, he mutters, "we must marry after this"—hardly the reaction of a man head over heels in love.

# CHAPTER 6: THE FIGURE AGAINST THE SKY

Hardy shifts his scene to give us a closer look at the figure who reappears at the top of the barrow. He emphasizes her mysteriousness, her concentration, her complete absence of fear in this wild and lonely place. The wind blowing through the dead heath-bells and the woman's deep sigh are linked as symbols of lost happiness. She looks through a telescope at Wildeve's window far below. Then, ignoring her watch, she looks to see that the sands of an hourglass she carries have run out. This is another haunting symbol of loss, of things coming to an end.

She heads home, dazed and seemingly distressed. A weary small boy tending the bonfire beside her house calls her by name—Eustacia. We finally hear her speak, after this long build-up, and what we hear is tension, determination, selfishness, guile. Although both her grandfather and the boy, Johnny want Eustacia to put out her bonfire, she imperiously insists on keeping it burning—and she gets her way. Why does it matter so much to her? Soon we learn that the fire is meant to attract Wildeve. Eustacia warns Johnny to call her if he hears a frog jump into a pond nearby. When he does hear such a sound, Eustacia excitedly packs him off home, for the hop-frog is really a stone falling into the water, Wildeve's signal to Eustacia. To her "triumphant pleasure," he emerges out of the dark night.

The drama of their confrontation is skillfully muted. Each of these extremely passionate characters tries to suppress his or her emotion. Slowly, we learn the truth about their shared past. Damon had tired of her, we learn, and had ended their affair. But now Eustacia believes that Wildeve has broken off his wedding with Thomasin because he still loves her, Eustacia. When pressed, he agrees.

Is Wildeve lying? Can he change his mind so quickly? Does Eustacia have a dangerous power over him? The answer is complex. Hardy is showing us characters who let their impulses carry them away. Each of them is uneasy. Eustacia knows her former lover is untrustworthy; he knows her moods and pays no attention when she rages at him.

This uncomfortable scene ends with each holding back from the other, pretending to be less emotionally involved than the other. There is hostility, not flirtation, in their teasing. Wildeve slinks back into the night. The pleasure Eustacia felt when she first saw him has soured.

## CHAPTER 7: QUEEN OF NIGHT

Many critics, frankly, have found this short chapter to be an embarrassment. It has no purpose but to describe Eustacia in terms that are extravagant and pretentious. If you're interested in how a writer develops, this chapter is a good example, at least of Hardy's case. The first part of the book has many passages of strained "purple" prose like this. As he wrote this novel, however, Hardy learned more of his craft, and his writing grows simpler and more effective.

The chapter does help us understand Hardy's intentions in creating Eustacia. She is a pagan, a creature of the night, a kind of goddess in human form. Unfortunately, she is a goddess rudely brought to earth—to Egdon, so different from her nature.

Eustacia has romance in her veins and in her upbringing. We learn that she is the orphan of an

English mother (Vye's daughter) and a Greek musician. Their deaths forced her to leave the seaside resort, Budmouth, to live with Vye in Egdon. The heath bores her, and she imagines her earlier life, by contrast, as nothing but sunshine and gaiety.

We also learn that Eustacia is in love with love. This is a common human feeling, of course, but Eustacia takes it to extremes. She blames her own reckless, unconventional spirit on the fact that she's been disappointed by a cruel destiny. She realizes, in a moment of self-honesty, that she has fastened upon Wildeve simply for lack of anyone better.

So far, Eustacia doesn't seem to be a very appealing human being. Yet Hardy says that she is "not altogether unlovable" at times. Many readers agree. Why do you sympathize with this self-centered, reckless young woman (if you do)? What makes her interesting (if you think she is)? As you read on, try to decide what elements of her character really define her.

## CHAPTER 8: THOSE WHO ARE FOUND WHERE THERE IS SAID TO BE NOBODY

Remember that the action is still taking place at night. As readers, we are still "in the dark" about certain things. So, too, are the characters of the story. Hardy may well be implying that people are always in darkness about the real truths of their lives.

In any event, poor Johnny now finds himself in a dark and difficult position. Walking home, he notices a peculiar light and puzzling sounds rising from a pit. He turns back to the Vyes' house, but sees Eustacia and Wildeve having their tryst, so he returns to the pit, where he discovers Diggory Venn, a terrifying image with his white eyes and teeth gleaming in his reddened face. Diggory discovers Johnny, who says enough for Venn to guess the truth about Eustacia's bonfire meeting with Wildeve.

The reddleman's thoughts are not explicitly revealed, but we can guess that he means to keep an eye on this secret relationship. Is he acting out of selfish motives, or does he just want to make sure that Thomasin is not hurt any further? Perhaps Hardy himself wasn't sure, at least at this point.

We can be sure of one thing, though. Chance, once again, has played a critical role. Johnny accidentally overhead the conversation. Diggory accidentally heard the story from the boy.

---

NOTE:  Venn as Observer      It is often the outsider, the social outcast, who is able to understand more than other people. The reddleman is an observer, not a major actor; and as he watches the other characters' actions, he alone seems to foresee how they may be ruining their lives. In the eyes of the superstitious, he seems to be a devil, the embodiment of evil. But appearances, in Hardy's world, are deceiving. To the reader, Diggory Venn is more likely to become a symbol of good.

---

## CHAPTER 9: LOVE LEADS A SHREWD MAN INTO STRATEGY

Hardy begins this chapter with a break in the action, perhaps to let the events and revelations of the preceding pages sink in on the reader. This break is not just an intermission, however. The novelist explains more about reddlemen, which brings us to

Venn, back at his van in the pit, who does not fit the pattern. We watch him read an old letter—Thomasin's polite refusal of his proposal of marriage. Her reasons were that she liked but did not love him, and that her aunt had higher ambitions for her. Remember that Mrs. Yeobright also opposed Wildeve's proposal. How different would things be if Thomasin allowed herself to act on her own best impulses? Remember that she is young, unsophisticated, and basically well intentioned. As we read further, circumstances will be bringing her to greater maturity.

Meanwhile, we learn that Diggory became a reddleman, giving up his dairy farm, because of Thomasin's rejection. But he is still determined to help her to be happy. With that aim in mind, he becomes something of a spy, waiting every night to catch Eustacia and Wildeve meeting again.

After a week, they do. Diggory hides himself to overhear their disturbing discussion. Wildeve, to Eustacia's outrage, is asking her whether or not he should go ahead and marry Thomasin—not out of love but to save the girl from disgrace. Eustacia advises him not to marry Thomasin simply out of a sense of justice, but she now realizes that Wildeve did not call off the marriage for love of her. As he admits, it was only chance that the marriage license was incorrect.

In this scene, Wildeve is shown at his worst: self-centered, weak, moody. He has the gall to tell Eustacia that "there are two flowers where I thought there was only one"—Eustacia and Thomasin. Perhaps other women will love him as well, he muses. As for love, he admits that his feelings are inconstant. Eustacia, stretched on the rack by this indifference, shows remarkable self-control.

---

**NOTE: Eustacia's and Wildeve's Love**     Hardy
never shows us these lovers when their love is in full
summer bloom. We see the wreckage—bitterness,
misunderstanding, petty cruelty. Perhaps the love
they shared cannot really be put down on the page;
perhaps Hardy purposely leaves room for each of us
to imagine his or her own rare, blinding, whirlwind
love. Or perhaps Hardy is simply more interested in
investigating and dissecting a failed relationship. You
may want to consider this possibility as you read
about other relationships later in the novel.

---

We now see two people who are tortured by inability to live without—or with—each other. Each of the
lovers wavers between love and distaste for the other.
When one goes too far, the other retreats. They do
agree that they hate the heath, however. Suddenly,
Wildeve suggests that they run off to America together; he has relatives in Wisconsin. Eustacia turns
the idea aside, for the moment. They move out of
Diggory's hearing, almost seeming to sink into the
heath, as if it has them in its power. Diggory, concerned for Thomasin's welfare, decides he will have it
out with Eustacia.

## CHAPTER 10: A DESPERATE ATTEMPT
## AT PERSUASION

At last, we see daylight in Egdon. Diggory waits
patiently by Eustacia's cottage until curiosity brings
her outside. As they walk, he tries a simple ruse. Pretending that an unknown "other woman" has a hold
over Wildeve, he asks Eustacia to use her charms to
persuade the man to marry Thomasin honorably.
Eustacia laughs off the suggestion.

Next Venn tries flattery; he says that Eustacia's beauty will influence woman-loving Wildeve to do the proper thing. When she reacts with the blatant lie that she never sees Wildeve, Diggory blurts out that he overheard their rendezvous the night before.

Now that the cards are on the table, Eustacia and the reddleman speak frankly. She refuses to yield to Thomasin; she blames her boredom here on Egdon heath for making her ever fall in love with Wildeve. Diggory, proposes a solution; he knows of a wealthy widow in Eustacia's treasured town of Budmouth. Eustacia could live with this woman, as her companion thereby escaping the heath and meeting more suitable men. Eustacia rejects the notion, refuses to help Thomasin, and dismisses Venn with insults.

Eustacia looks off toward Wildeve's inn, shining attractively in the sunlight. She is hooked again, because the competition from Thomasin has turned a "hobby" into a flood of desire.

And what about society's disapproval? Hardy notes that this young woman is too isolated to care about public opinion. This chapter is the second time someone has suggested a plan of escape from the heath she despises, but Eustacia refuses this offer, just as she passed over Wildeve's idea of eloping to Wisconsin.

---

**NOTE: Eustacia's Inability to Escape**     Perhaps Hardy believes that even independent people are unable to take action to change their fate. The heath has some power over Eustacia, that neither she nor the reader can fully understand. Maybe its mystery draws her. Maybe she realizes that these chances of "escape" will only create new prisons for her. Or maybe Eustacia isn't as independent as she thinks she is; Hardy's characters, like people in real life, don't always see themselves clearly.

## CHAPTER 11: THE DISHONESTY OF AN HONEST WOMAN

By the kind of accident familiar to us by now, Diggory bumps into Mrs. Yeobright just as she heads toward The Quiet Woman, hoping to convince Wildeve to go through with the aborted marriage. Ironically, the reddleman gives her just the weapon she needs. He confesses his love for Thomasin and argues that marriage to him would solve the situation. Mrs. Yeobright argues that Thomasin must be married to Wildeve to avoid scandal. But when she meets with Wildeve, she announces that Thomasin has an anonymous other suitor, and that Wildeve should either marry Thomasin immediately or give her up. Typically, indecisive Wildeve says he must take a day or two to decide.

**NOTE: On Wildeve** Consider this man for a moment. He is not actively evil or openly vicious. Yet all three of these strong women have humbled themselves before him. He rarely seems to be purposely cruel, but his weakness and self-centeredness often have cruel effects upon women. His sensuality makes him dangerous. Perhaps Hardy is saying that it is well to distrust the objects of passion, just as one should be wary of passion itself.

Mrs. Yeobright's ultimatum motivates Wildeve to make a nighttime visit to Eustacia. He impetuously repeats the offer to take her to America, but he lets the cat out of the bag, telling Eustacia that Thomasin has another offer. Instantly, Eustacia's attitude changes: the man who was so desirable is less so when her rival may no longer want him. Wildeve realizes what she is thinking, perhaps because this is the way his mind works as well. In any case, Eustacia becomes oddly lifeless. Almost bargaining now, Wildeve offers her a week to decide. Coldly, the lovers part. Eustacia, who always tries to face her feelings with honesty, is ashamed to find her passion waning because there is no competition. But she sees that the affair is dying; she is coming to her senses at last.

Unexpectedly, the chapter (and Book First) ends with a new twist in the action which arouses our curiosity about the book to follow. While drinking and gossiping down at The Quiet Woman, Captain Vye has heard that Mrs. Yeobright's son, Clym, is coming home the following week for Christmas. He tells Eustacia this news, explaining that the young man has been living "in that rookery of pomp and vanity, Paris . . . "

Hardy does not describe Eustacia's reaction, but every reader knows, from this wonderfully pregnant closing line, that her heart must have leapt into her mouth. If little Budmouth seems magical to Eustacia, how must the world-famed City of Light appear? We know her love for Wildeve is almost dead. She has said she only loved him because no better man was to be found in the area. Now, there appears on the horizon a tantalizing alternative. Skillfully, by saying no more, Hardy has raised our hopes, too. Perhaps Clym will be the answer to Eustacia's loneliness.

We're not likely to be too optimistic, though, after this chapter, for we have seen two fairly pessimistic Hardy themes. First, we saw that people's actions don't always have the consequences they intend. Diggory's offer of marriage, if anything, helped to throw Wildeve and Thomasin together. Mrs. Yeobright's threats had the unexpected effect of driving Wildeve swiftly back to Eustacia. Second, we've seen that people often desire something primarily because they can't have it. Often, when we get what we want, it is no longer desirable.

# BOOK TWO: THE ARRIVAL

The first book has been the longest, perhaps necessarily so in order to set the background for the central action of the novel. In this book, we will meet the last of the major characters, Clym Yeobright.

## CHAPTER 1: TIDINGS OF THE COMER

Drawing out our anticipation, Hardy does not introduce Clym right away. Instead, we see the humble furze-gatherers of the heath at work stacking up the furze, or sticks of wood, for Captain Vye. (Such men are socially beneath Eustacia—a point which will be important later on.)

Now, Hardy lets Eustacia idly overhear these men gossip about young Yeobright—his success in the diamond business, his good looks, his advanced ideas and education. Innocently, the furze-gatherers leap to the notion that Eustacia, who also reads a great deal, would be a good match for Clym. We also learn that the story of Thomasin's postponed marriage is now common knowledge around Egdon. She is in seclusion, and there is talk that she has decided to have nothing more to do with Wildeve.

As Hardy notes, this idle chatter has occupied only a few minutes. To the transfixed Eustacia, however, it has been enough to re-animate her world. She is dazed by the possibilities. A young, clever, successful man who might take her to fabled Paris? A man whom the country folk already see as similar to her? This must be fate. Not surprisingly, the chapter ends with her taking a walk to Blooms-End, the Yeobright family cottage.

She doesn't expect to see Clym himself, but, already dangerously fascinated, she at least wants to see the house where he was born. Her romantic imagination is working at full strength again. The headstrong 19-year-old who once swore passionately that she would never give up Wildeve is now concentrating all her thoughts on a man she has never even met.

## CHAPTER 2: THE PEOPLE AT BLOOMS-END MAKE READY

The return of the native Clym is a major event in sleepy Egdon. Thomasin and Mrs. Yeobright discuss Clym as they meticulously select from storage the apples he likes best. Apparently, Mrs. Yeobright once hoped Thomasin and Clym would marry, we learn. Then, when no one is around to stare (remember Thomasin is still in shamed seclusion), they venture out on the heath to pick holly berries for the homecoming and Christmas celebrations.

As they work, their conversation takes many frustrating dead-ends. Mrs. Yeobright suspects that her niece no longer loves Wildeve, but Thomasin decides not to answer any questions about the matter. Mrs. Yeobright has decided not to reveal that Diggory has proposed again, although she does drop a hint. Thomasin decides that her cousin Clym should not be told anything about the wretched affair until she is safely married.

Don't you want to jump into the scene and interfere? We sense that these decisions are mistaken. Perhaps Thomasin, if she knew of the proposal, would consider marrying the kindly, selfless Venn rather than egocentric Wildeve, after what she's been through. Perhaps Clym, who is so clever, would help her figure out whether or not to marry Wildeve. There is nothing we can do, of course. We must watch helplessly as people make mistakes that will haunt them for years, if not forever.

Appropriately, the sun is setting as Thomasin and her aunt walk out to meet Clym on the road. Once again, important events will take place during the dark of night.

## CHAPTER 3: HOW A LITTLE SOUND PRODUCED A GREAT DREAM

By another coincidence, in the darkness, Eustacia encounters Clym and his two relatives. They apparently don't recognize her, but Clym genially says, "Good night!" It is, as the chapter title indicates, truly a "little sound," but to Eustacia, "no event could have been more exciting." There is one slightly unsettling note—she overhears Clym, the sophisticate, praising the beauties of Egdon. The remark is an important clue to her fate, but she is too excited to pay attention to it now. At home, Eustacia asks her grandfather why they haven't been on good terms with the Yeobrights. He recalls that he offended Mrs. Yeobright once; more importantly, he tells Eustacia that the Yeobrights' mode of living is "countrified." This is the second indication that Clym is not what Eustacia imagines him to be. But she pays no attention; she still cherishes her illusions.

**NOTE: Eustacia's Dream**    That night Eustacia dreams of dancing with a man whose face is masked by a helmet. The heath appears behind them, and they dive into one of its pools, coming out beneath in a hollow lit with rainbows. She wakes up with alarm when the man shatters to pieces, never having revealed his face. She believes the figure was Yeobright, of course. But remember this dream; as you will see at the end of the fifth book, another more frightening interpretation is possible.

---

Hardy describes Eustacia's emotional state as in a precarious stage, halfway between indifference and love. She begins taking walks two or three times a day, her eyes peeled for a glimpse of Yeobright, but after five days of failure she gives up. Hardy ends the chapter with the observation that Fate (or Providence) sometimes likes to tease us, hinting that Eustacia will soon have the opportunity she has given up on. When she does finally meet Clym, therefore, it will not be entirely her own doing. Fate, Hardy emphasizes, will play a role.

# CHAPTER 4: EUSTACIA IS LED ON TO AN ADVENTURE

Once again, Hardy stresses a date. The novel began on November 5; now it is December 23 and everyone is preparing for Christmas. By using holidays, Hardy has an opportunity to bring many elements of the community together so that we can see the whole spectrum of rural life.

At the beginning of the chapter, however, he focuses on Eustacia's frustration at not meeting Clym. A scheme does present itself, however. Bursting in on

the pensive Eustacia, Charley, a young lad, announces that he and some other amateur actors have
come to practice their parts for the annual Christmas
play in Captain Vye's fuel-house. Eustacia is at first
uninterested, but when the sound of rehearsal
reaches her bored ears, she slips outside to eavesdrop.
By chance, she learns from the players' conversation
that their first performance of the holiday will take
place at Mrs. Yeobright's home. Clym will be at the
party, of course, but Eustacia has not been invited.

Later, when Charley enters to return the key, she
has hatched a plan. Aware that the boy is dazzled by
her, she asks him to let her play his role, the Turkish
knight, for the appearance at Blooms-End, keeping it
a secret from everyone else. Eustacia offers to pay for
this, but Charley strikes a peculiar bargain. He will
agree if she lets him kiss her hand and hold it for
fifteen minutes. Charley's adoration reminds us, at
this crucial point, how irresistable Eustacia can be.

The next evening, when the boy returns with his
medieval costume, Eustacia indifferently lets him
hold her hand for a few of the bargained-for minutes.
Then she dresses as the Turkish knight and runs
through her lines in front of Charley. She explains
that she will simply show up in his place, already
dressed in her disguise, and claim to be his cousin,
saying that he's been sent on an errand by Eustacia
Vye.

The chapter ends on a strange, touching note.
Charley asks for another minute of holding Eustacia's
hand; he can't bear to pull away and his time is fully
used up to his regret. In his own meager way, Charley, too, gives in to passion. His lack of control mirrors
Eustacia's much more extravagant lack of control.
What about her feelings in this scene? Is she embar-

assed by Charley's request? Characteristically, she
ides her feelings. What we do see is that, when she
ets her mind on something, she will not let minor
obstacles (such as conventional ideas of behavior)
stand in the way. To see Clym, she'll fulfill Charley's
pathetic request. She will also disguise herself as a
man. Some readers think this is an indication that
she takes the male role, the dominant role, when she
meets Clym. Others think it simply shows that she
does not care what society thinks.

## CHAPTER 5: THROUGH THE MOONLIGHT

Like the helmeted figure in her dream that ended as
a nightmare, Eustacia has her visor down when she
shows up in Charley's place the next night. When
they arrive at Blooms-End, the mummers must wait
outside while a boisterous party is in full swing.
Hardy obviously enjoys giving the details of the rustic
music and dancing, but the merrymaking goes on a
bit too long for the waiting mummers. When someone suggests that they interrupt the party, Eustacia
reacts angrily—and gives her identity away. The players, however, amiably promise to keep her secret.

Finally, the group is admitted, and the play begins.
As the Turkish knight, Eustacia declaims her melodra-
matic lines, slays the Valiant Soldier, and is in turn
dispatched by the hero, St. George, the patron saint of
England. This dramatic defeat, however, gives her the
opportunity she's been seeking. During her performance, she was unable to concentrate on the audi-
ence. Now, as a corpse, Eustacia can lie still and scan
the crowd to find the face she is so eager to see. The
suspense is heightened, for she is still searching as the
chapter ends.

**NOTE:   Social Class in Egdon**        Notice the obser
vations Hardy makes about social class in this chapter
When Eustacia snaps at her cohorts, both she and
they accept that she is socially superior to them, with
out feeling any resentment. Eustacia is surprised that
the party is so rowdy, but we learn that the Yeobright
have asked all their neighbours, not just the social
elite. Clym and his mother even serve these guest
themselves. Their graciousness and hospitality is con
trasted to Eustacia's self-contained, isolated haughti
ness. Yet the social distance between the Yeobright
and the humbler folk of Egdon is not lessened; the
social order does not change easily in these pre
industrial rural towns.

# CHAPTER 6: THE TWO STAND FACE TO FACE

As the play of St. George continues, Eustacia in
tently surveys the room. (Sadly, we note that Thom
asin is upstairs, too ashamed to face her neighbors.
Eustacia is soon riveted by her first sight of Clym's
face, lit by firelight as if he is a figure in a Rembrandt
painting. Like the famous Dutch artist, Hardy uses
physical details to reveal the character's inner nature.
Clym's young face already shows experience beyond
his years. Thought, Hardy warns, will soon destroy
his handsomeness; his natural cheerfulness is at war
with the depressing knowledge that he is gaining of
the world. The novelist also points out that Clym's
look shows "isolation"—and Eustacia, that other iso
lated person, is very much moved.

When the play ends, the country folk pay their
respects to Clym. Clearly, Humphrey and the others
deeply admire the young man. Overall, we feel the

usual festive atmosphere of people whose lives are deeply intertwined.

Meanwhile, Eustacia has a problem: she can't eat with her helmet on, but she wants to keep her identity concealed. Clym, as host, tries to serve her. Imagine her strange situation. The man she is "determined to love" is being kind to her, but without knowing who she is. Clym, however, begins to suspect something about this young mummer.

Suddenly, as only Eustacia notices, Thomasin appears to ask Clym about something. Eustacia overhears just enough of the conversation to learn that Clym doesn't know about Thomasin's painful situation. From fantasy Eustacia is brought back to earth; her jealousy of Thomasin flares anew. She wonders if the cousins will fall in love, especially since they spend so much time alone together.

Ironically, Eustacia's ruse has deprived her of a powerful weapon, her feminine beauty. But now Clym has begun staring at her. Confused, she quietly slips out of the house into the moonlight. Clym, having guessed her sex, is right behind her. She admits that she is a woman, offering no other information, and refuses his invitation to return to the party.

The conversation is brief, but important. Eustacia's answers are straightforward and direct: her adventure was meant as an escape from the depression which "Life"causes for her. In their first meeting, Eustacia explains herself to Clym with complete honesty. He listens without seeming to be surprised or critical. There seems to be instant communication between them.

When Eustacia leaves, Clym walks up and down for a while by himself, apparently lost in thought. Eustacia too is in mental turmoil—happy, fearful, ashamed, jealous. When she nears home and catches sight of Rainbarrow, she remembers for the first time this evening that she had asked Wildeve to meet her up there—but it is too late now. She feels no remorse for standing him up; at this point, he means nothing to her. In fact, she wishes that she hadn't stopped him from marrying Thomasin; then there would be no dangerous competition for Clym.

Hardy's point is that one can never predict the outcome of events. Eustacia interfered with the Wildeve's marriage because he seemed to be her one hope at the time. She could not know that a more appealing man would soon appear. The future, Hardy shows us, is unpredictable; therefore man's attempts to control his own destiny are doomed to be futile.

## CHAPTER 7: A COALITION BETWEEN BEAUTY AND ODDNESS

The next morning, Captain Vye uncharacteristically asks his granddaughter why she'd been out so late. He is delighted to hear about the trick she played. He warns that once is enough, however, to go around in breeches. It is very odd for a woman of this time and place to act as freely as she does.

Eustacia wanders off again, only to run upon Diggory. He is hanging around because of Thomasin, it seems; other reddlemen have gone off for the winter. Eustacia has already guessed that Venn is Wildeve's supposed rival, and, like Mrs. Yeobright, she now wants no obstacle placed between Thomasin and Wildeve. When Wildeve appears in the distance Eustacia hides inside Diggory's van. Eventually, she convinces Diggory that she no longer cares for Wildeve. As it happens, Venn was watching the night before when Wildeve, angrily waiting on the barrow, vowed to return at the same time this night. Eustacia asks Diggory to take a message to Wildeve, because she doesn't want to see him again. She is puzzled that Diggory agrees. Why should he carry news that will make his rival marry Thomasin at last? Eustacia just can't understand Diggory's unselfish love.

Hardy's irony here is significant. What we commonly call love may only be self-centeredness. So far in this novel, only Diggory has shown another kind of love. He is sometimes linked with satanic images, but at other times he seems to be more like an angel.

In any event, he brings Eustacia's farewell letter to the barrow that night, startling the already distraught Wildeve. Annoyed, Wildeve reveals that he knows Diggory is his rival. The two men quickly part, each to mull over his own muddled situation.

Wildeve thinks Eustacia is only pretending to break it off with him; he decides to punish her by marrying Thomasin as quickly as possible. Diggory, equally fired to action, dresses himself in a good suit (although the red dye remains on his face) and rushes off to Blooms-End. But he is too late. Wildeve emerges from the Yeobright cottage, gloating, Obviously, Thomasin has accepted him. Diggory goes back to his van and puts on his working clothes. Returning to his life as a reddleman he is symbolically returning to his state of rejection by Thomasin. Wildeve, it seems, has won. But what has he won? His motives for marrying Thomasin seem flimsy and hasty; we may also wonder why Thomasin is marrying him—for love, or out of cowardice? Hardy has made clear that this marriage is doomed. Thinking to free herself, Eustacia has unwittingly set off unhappy changes in the lives of several people.

# CHAPTER 8: FIRMNESS IS DISCOVERED IN A GENTLE HEART

Hardy backs up to show us the end of the previous chapter from another view—inside the Yeobright cottage. Thomasin explains to her aunt why she has accepted Wildeve's proposal—not because of passion, but because "I am a practical woman now. I don't believe in hearts at all." Mrs. Yeobright leaves and comes back with the news that Diggory has also proposed, but Thomasin hardly gives him a thought.

The next day, bravely dressing herself up as if the occasion were joyous, Thomasin walks off alone toward the church of another parish. In a burst of feeling, she rushes back and hugs her aunt tearfully. Thomasin sets off firmly in a moment, however, crossing the heath "solitary and undefended."

Some time later, Clym appears, and his mother now reveals the whole story. He is surprised, though he's heard rumors already, but he reacts rather casually. Is he a forgiving man, or simply a man of mild feelings? He shows no anger toward Wildeve; he doesn't consider whether the marriage can be happy, under the circumstances. He lightly recalls that he was attracted to Thomasin when they were younger, although he seems to dismiss it as a childhood crush now. Hardy is beginning to shift our attention from Thomasin to Clym; pay attention to these first clues to his character.

Clym decides he must go to the wedding out of kindness. But he returns within minutes, accompanied by Diggory, who reports that Wildeve arrived on time and the pair have been married at last. He has an astonishing detail to add: Eustacia Vye was there to give the bride away. Clym, who doesn't connect her with the mysterious Turkish knight, asks who that is. His aunt mentions the local superstition that the girl is a witch. Though she scoffs, perhaps we feel it's partly true. Eustacia does have a power to bewitch men, a skill she means to work on Clym himself.

What Diggory doesn't reveal is that Eustacia had asked him to warn her when the wedding was about to take place. Veiled, she hung about the church as a stranger, until she was asked to witness the ceremony. Only after the ceremony did she show herself to Wildeve and Thomasin. Hardy then backtracks to the wedding to show us a significant detail that Diggory did not notice. Wildeve and Eustacia, knowing each other so well, exchange intense glances, each feeling triumphant over the other. The question Hardy lets hang, unspoken, is whether either has really won.

---

**NOTE: Darkness and Light**    This dramatic confrontation at Wildeve's wedding shows Eustacia once again hiding herself, this time with a veil. Before, she hid from Wildeve in Diggory's van. At Blooms-End, she wore a helmet. At her grandfather's cottage, she overheard useful conversations by staying out of sight. Perhaps this is Hardy's way of adding to her mystery. Just as she conceals her face, she often conceals her feelings. She also follows her desires, even when they are unconscious, or "hidden" from her. Perhaps, for Hardy, passionate feelings are the dark side of the soul. Eustacia seems to thrive in darkness. Clym, on the other hand, has already been identified with images of light. Reason, as opposed to passion, is often symbolized by light.

---

# BOOK THREE:
# THE FASCINATION

This title contains a very strong word. We use it
casually in conversation today, to express simple
attraction. In this book, however, Hardy portrays a
*fascination* that is almost like a supernatural spell.
Clym and Eustacia are tragically different kinds of
human beings, but when passion and idealism blind
them, they are swept away.

## CHAPTER 1: "MY MIND TO ME A KINGDOM IS"

The chapter begins with a close-up on Clym. Like
Eustacia, we still don't know much about this unusual
person. Now, Hardy elaborates upon his earlier comment that the young man's face is interesting because
it reveals experience. Life has already touched and
saddened him, perhaps.

We learn that Clym was a gifted child, famous
throughout the area. He was expected to become
either a great success or a great failure—nothing ordinary. Now, however, the country folk are puzzled.
For a successful Parisian businessman, Clym seems to
be taking a very long holiday.

At the local men's weekly hair-cutting outside Fairway's house, the gossip turns to this subject when
they see Clym rambling over the heath. Within
minutes, he walks up and guesses what they've been
talking about. Note how Hardy stresses Clym's con-
nection with the heath and his insight into other
human beings—up to a point.

Characteristically, Clym straightforwardly satisfies
the villagers' curiosity. In vain, idle Paris, he says, he

felt useless and depressingly out of place. Now, he has decided to educate himself at home and then start a rural school near Egdon.

Without waiting for a reaction, he goes back toward the heath, wrapped up in his own thoughts. The villagers think he's making a mistake. Ironically, they're the very class of people he's hoping to help.

Had Eustacia overheard this conversation, her hopes might have sunk. Once, Clym felt as she does that Egdon was contemptible; now, however, the sole ambition of his life is to live and work there.

Now we know what motivates Clym, as Eustacia unfortunately does not. We've seen the contrast between young Yeobright's idealism and the down-to-earth opinions of the men of Egdon. The stage is set for later conflicts. Perhaps the title of the chapter is Hardy's warning that Clym is living inside his own mind, dangerously supposing it to be the entire kingdom. That could prove to be a form of moral blindness.

## CHAPTER 2: THE NEW COURSE CAUSES DISAPPOINTMENT

**NOTE: Clym's Idealism**    Hardy explains the difficulty of Clym's position. He is too far ahead of his time. In Paris he was exposed to new ideas, among them the notion that education can elevate simple, uneducated people to noble heights. Clym has foolishly (in the eyes of his friends) abandoned his career for this. Hardy suggests that the young man might be either a madman or a prophet; in any case, Clym does not take the middle course of "happiness and mediocrity." The novelist also explains that Yeobright idealizes the heath, loving each thing that Eustacia hates. He's glad that attempts to tame the heath by farming it have all failed.

---

Returning to Blooms-End, Clym announces his plans to his mother; thus begins a classic confrontation, not to be resolved. A materialistic woman, Mrs. Yeobright believes that a man should try to succeed in business. Clym has come to believe that true manhood lies in helping mankind out of ignorance and misery.

Suddenly, the timid, superstitious Christian bursts in with a shocking story, almost as if to prove that Egdon is in desperate need of enlightenment. In church that morning, Johnny Nunsuch's mother, Susan, pricked Eustacia Vye with a needle, so hard that it drew blood and caused the girl to faint. Susan believes that Eustacia has bewitched the Nunsuch children. Cristian rattles on, enjoying his tale, but the Yeobrights instantly feel compassion for Eustacia. Even Clym is taken aback by this living example of backward rural behavior.

Humphrey and, later, another local, Sam, comes by to confirm the news. In addition, Sam refers to Eustacia as a "beauty," and Clym begins to suspect that Eustacia may have been the Turkish knight. Sam explains that he has stopped by to borrow some rope, to help retrieve Captain Vye's water bucket, which has dropped to the bottom of the well. Out of Mrs. Yeobright's hearing, Sam urges Clym to get a look at Eustacia; the gathering at the well would be a good excuse to drop by her cottage. Obviously, Clym is attracted, although not at all with the force of curiosity that drove Eustacia to join the mummers. For the moment, Hardy doesn't let us know exactly what the young man is thinking, although he is thinking "a good deal."

## CHAPTER 3: THE FIRST ACT IN A TIMEWORN DRAMA

After a sunny walk on the heath, the Yeobrights literally (and symbolically) take separate paths: Clym to Eustacia, his mother to Thomasin. Mrs. Yeobright, seeing his eagerness, is fearful of what may happen. She decides not to visit The Quiet Woman and worriedly returns home.

Fairway, the natural leader of the local men assembled around Captain Vye's well, has tried without success to bring up the bucket, but it slips off just at the top. Clym offers to try while Fairway rests. Suddenly, Eustacia shocks everyone by crying out, from an upper window of the cottage, that they must tie a rope around Clym because of the danger. Clym recognizes the voice of the mysterious woman he met by moonlight, and innocently thinks, "How thoughtful of her!" We, of course, have the advantage of knowing that her feelings go far deeper than mere thoughtfulness.

Eventually, the men give up for the night. Clym, left alone with Eustacia, offers to help her draw water from the well. Helping him, Eustacia hurts her hands on the rope; when Clym expresses concern, she also shows him the wound Susan Nunsuch left on her arm. Intimacy seems to have instantly flowered between these two unusual people.

Nonetheless, they may not be listening carefully enough to what each other exactly says. Eustacia is clearly appalled by the idea of teaching in Clym's school but Clym doesn't quite pay attention. Clym wants to live near Egdon more than anywhere else in the world, obviously including Paris, but Eustacia may not quite hear him. In this brief encounter, Hardy spells out the problems of communication that will dog this pair until the end.

Compare their reactions as they part. Eustacia thinks a completely new life has begun for her. Clym is so inspired, he immediately beings his studies—the very project which is in conflict with Eustacia's ambitions.

Clym works through the bright sunny day. In the evening, as he confesses to his mother, he meets Eustacia again. Mrs. Yeobright, though she's already reconciling herself to her son's new career, doesn't like this growing relationship—and says so. Clym implies that he has no romantic interest in Eustacia. Why is he hedging? Hardy discusses the love between mother and son—indestructible, even when it isn't openly affectionate. The Yeobrights understand each other, although they disagree. Eustacia will have a tough job trying to win Clym over his mother's wishes.

A few days later on, Christian reports to Mrs. Yeobright about an amateur archaeological dig in a barrow on the heath. Clym apparently took one of the artifacts and gave it to Eustacia, though as Mrs. Yeobright intuitively realizes, Clym had intended to bring it to his mother first. He must have acted on an impulse of the moment. Perhaps Eustacia may be replacing Mrs. Yeobright in Clym's affections, even though he may not yet fully realize it.

The weeks pass; Clym studies at home and frequently meets Eustacia on the heath. As March arrives, the heath begins to come back to life with the spring. So, too, does Clym, as love finally blossoms. He is even considering the possibility of marriage. In an angry conversation, Mrs. Yeobright accuses her son of using his teaching scheme to cover up his real reason for staying in Egdon—his fascination with Eustacia. Clym, however, actually visualizes Eustacia as "a good matron in a boarding-school." Mrs. Yeobright heatedly calls Eustacia a "hussy," but her son's red-faced reaction silences her. They part angrily. As Hardy warns us, this is the "first act" of a drama that is "timeworn."

---

**NOTE: Hardy's View of Marriage**     Does Hardy mean that all marriages are based upon such deep misunderstanding? Some readers think he believes successful marriages are certainly rare. As you read, you may want to look at other marriages in this novel. Decide for yourself how troubles arise in this doomed marriage: from the contradiction between the natures of Clym and Eustacia, or from the difficulty of marriage between any two people.

---

## CHAPTER 4: AN HOUR OF BLISS AND MANY HOURS OF SADNESS

As the chapter title indicates, Hardy leaves no doubt that things are going to turn out badly. The Yeobrights pass an uneasy day together. When it is dark, Clym leaves, to watch an eclipse of the moon atop Rainbarrow, but as the moon goes into shadow, we see him run down to meet Eustacia at the base of the barrow, where they kiss passionately. Passion, we remember, is in Hardy a thing of darkness. Clym says that he is in love for the first time in his life. Eustacia, who is more experienced in these matters, fears that this love "will evaporate like a spirit." She also recognizes, realistically, that Mrs. Yeobright would like these meetings to stop.

To all of her fears and objections, Clym has one answer: a proposal of marriage. Elusive Eustacia, however, won't agree. She'd rather hear about Paris. Clym doesn't like this topic, but he describes the city to her; bewitched by the vision, she promises to marry him—if he will take her there. He says he will never return. She doesn't believe him, but she finally consents to marry him, even though she's honest enough to realize she won't make much of a housewife.

Betrothed to each other at last, the lovers part on a strangely sad note. Eustacia remembers that she once fell madly in love at the mere glimpse of a stranger. She knows that her love for Clym may be fragile. He, despite the intensity of his love, is troubled by her desire to go to Paris and by the breach growing between him and his mother. He wants to keep alive three things at once: Mrs. Yeobright's trust, his teaching scheme, Eustacia's happiness. But by their very natures, these three things will not co-exist.

---

**NOTE   The Meaning of the Eclipse**   The eclipse of the moon, a rare natural phenomenon, probably symbolizes another phenomenon rare in this novel—"an hour of bliss." All too briefly, the lovers have had an ecstatic encounter on the heath. Even in their happiness, each saw the difficulties before them. Neither, however, wants to turn back now, no matter what.

---

## CHAPTER 5: SHARP WORDS ARE SPOKEN, AND A CRISIS ENSUES

Clym's life now is centered on two activities only—his studies and his secret meetings with Eustacia. Then Mrs. Yeobright hears from Thomasin that

Captain Vye has announced Eustacia's engagement to Clym at The Quiet Woman. The stunned mother realizes that she has lost her son, but, hopeless as it is, she argues with him. The same old points are brought up again: she even mentions the rumor about Eustacia's affair with Wildeve, but Clym has already heard, and believed, his beloved's sanitized version of that episode. Clym announces that he and his bride will not go to Paris, but he will compromise by starting a school in Budmouth, the resort town Eustacia remembers from childhood.

Like many crucial arguments between people who are important to each other, this one darts from point to point; there is more stress than logic evident. Frantic Mrs. Yeobright says that she wishes Clym would leave the house, though she does not really mean it. Deeply hurt, he leaves, barely able to speak. As he walks away, however, the sunny afternoon seems to promise summer, much as his engagement, in his eyes, promises happiness.

He waits for Eustacia in a verdant hollow filled only with ferns, as if he and she will be alone at the beginning of the world. Sadly, this meeting was originally planned for Clym and Eustacia to win Mrs. Yeobright over to their plans. Eustacia, perceptively, guesses what has happened with Mrs. Yeobright yet she accepts this trouble philosophically. The lovers forget the world for a while, it seems, as they stroll through the tall ferns.

As this peaceful interlude comes to an end, the sun is about to set. Perhaps moved by the symbolism of the dying day, Eustacia exclaims that she cannot bear to part with Clym. Mirroring her passion, he decides they will get married immediately. Eustacia agrees, but notice her reaction when he explains that they will have to live in a tiny cottage on the heath until he's ready to take her to Budmouth. "How long . . . ?" is her question. Six months, he promises. Ominously, the marriage that was to be an escape from Egdon for her is beginning as no change at all, or even a setback, to life in a smaller, meaner house. Clym brightly promises that everything will work out. The decision has been made; they will marry in two weeks.

As Eustacia walks away, Clym feels a surprising stab of depression as he gazes at his beloved heath. Its bare flatness seems to suggest to him that he is not superior to anyone else. Despite his great desire to help the uneducated masses, he has just made the kind of mistake anyone might make. Eustacia, too, seems no longer a goddess to him but merely a woman. Reality is moving in.

Hardy ends this chapter by suggesting that the reality of marriage may not be to Eustacia's liking. Is Mrs. Yeobright's anger responsible for the couple's decision to marry right away? It is a factor, but so is the impatience of young love. By now, we're aware of many reasons why Clym and Eustacia should *not* marry. But it's difficult to imagine how anything could prevent this marriage. Passion has overpowered reason.

## CHAPTER 6: YEOBRIGHT GOES, AND THE BREACH IS COMPLETE

On a cold June day, Clym packs his goods and, without a word to his mother, goes off to rent a small cottage six miles away, where he will live alone until the wedding.

---

**NOTE: Pathetic Fallacy**     Notice how the weather seems to reflect Clym's mood. This is a literary technique called "pathetic fallacy," and you will find Hardy using it a lot. Clym also notes that some trees planted the year he was born are being battered by the wind—perhaps as he is being emotionally battered. Egdon heath itself, however, is hardly affected by the storm.

---

Left to herself, Mrs. Yeobright is distraught with grief. The next day, Thomasin appears—like a bird—and despite everything, she lights up the area by her presence. She says that her marriage is proceeding well enough, but she does have difficulty asking Wildeve for money. Mrs. Yeobright reveals that her husband left some money to be divided between Thomasin and Clym. She will give Thomasin her share on one condition: the girl must first see whether Wildeve will offer to give her any. Thomasin now tries to get her aunt to forgive Clym, but the older woman, for all her common sense, still feels hurt by his behavior. Thomasin visits her daily for a week to comfort her, but then is kept home by an unexplained illness.

We haven't seen Wildeve since the day of his wedding; now he appears again standing outside The Quiet Woman. A cart driver passes by with news of wedding preparations at Captain Vye's cottage. Wildeve's immediate reaction is a painful longing for Eustacia again. Why? Because another man wants her. Eustacia had a similar reaction toward Wildeve when Thomasin was her rival. Eustacia and Wildeve still resemble each other, it seems. Hardy scoffs at

Wildeve and at all people who indulge themselves by wanting only what they cannot have. He, like Eustacia, is the opposite of Clym, who loves what is near, in Egdon.

## CHAPTER 7: THE MORNING AND THE EVENING OF A DAY

Purposely, Hardy does not take us to Clym and Eustacia's wedding. Instead, we experience it only through the gloomy imaginings of Mrs. Yeobright. The day is lovely, and church bells peal merrily in the distance, but we are with a weeping woman who predicts her son will someday be sorry.

Later, Wildeve comes to Blooms-End. He and Thomasin's aunt seem to have made a necessary truce; he has made an effort to be courteous to her. But it appears that she still doesn't really trust him. Thomasin, who is at Clym's wedding at Mistover, has asked her husband to pick up "some article or other" from her aunt; she didn't explain to him that the "article" is her half of the money left by the late Mr. Yeobright. Mrs. Yeobright doesn't explain, either, but offends Wildeve by insisting on giving it to her niece in person.

After he leaves, Mrs. Yeobright decides to send the money to Thomasin at the wedding feast so that Wildeve won't find out about it. She'll send Clym's share at the same time, as a token of her good feeling for him. She divides the hundred guineas equally into two small canvas bags.

Unfortunately, she asks Christian, who is loitering about, to deliver the inheritance. On the way to Mistover, hearing voices over a rise, timid Christian empties the coins into his boots for safekeeping. The voices turn out by chance to be old friends, however, headed for a raffle at The Quiet Woman. Even though the prize is "a gown-piece for his wife or sweetheart," Christian, the man no woman could love, tags along, pathetically hoping to see the fun.

In fact, to the amusement of everyone at the inn, he does win the raffle. As the crowd starts carousing, Christian muses over his good fortune, superstitiously believing it proves that he was born lucky.

---

**NOTE: The Illusion of Good Fortune** Christian's foolish attitude toward the lucky dice could be an example of some common attitudes toward Fate. Hardy may be saying that, in times of good fortune, we are tempted to think we're in control of events. But the truth is probably otherwise, as Christian's actions soon show.

---

Christian stupidly drops enough hints for Wildeve to guess the nature of his errand to Mistover. Thomasin's husband, quickly setting a trap, offers to accompany Christian, and he lets him borrow a pair of those marvelous dice. As the two set out carrying a lantern, we learn that Diggory has been silently watching from the inn's dark chimney-corner.

Out in the warm misty night, Wildeve suggests a brief rest and a dice game. Christian, obsessed with the dice, is eager to try his newfound luck again. First Christian loses his own money. He decides to win it back by betting with Thomasin's money, but Wildeve wins the whole fifty guineas. Christian dips into Clym's share as well, but beyond control, that, too, is eventually lost.

Christian is struck with remorse, but Wildeve views the matter coolly. Even when he learns that half his winnings had actually belonged to Clym, he insists that he has gained fair possession of them. In his eyes, he hasn't committed a crime; he has merely proved his cleverness. Hardy, however, seems to feel Wildeve's behavior is not wholly admirable.

As the chapter ends, the defeated Christian totters away. Wildeve is about to leave, too, when Diggory suddenly appears in the light of the lantern. What does he know? What can he do? Hardy leaves the answers to the following chapter.

## CHAPTER 8: A NEW FORCE DISTURBS THE CURRENT

The "current" of the title probably refers to the trend of events, which, for the previous few pages, has turned in Wildeve's favor. In Hardy's world, however fate is not constant.

With no ceremony, Diggory sets down a coin; Wildeve cannot resist continuing to play. He obviously felt superior to Christian's naive eagerness, but now he is just as greedy and obsessed himself.

The game is tense, see-sawing back and forth. The two men make a contrast in temperament: "nervous and excitable" Wildeve, Diggory seeming like "a red-sandstone statue." Hardy clearly prefers Diggory; unlike many novelists, he often lets you know just how he feels about his characters.

Almost uncannily, Diggory begins to win. The furious Wildeve throws the dice away in frustration but insists that the game continue, even though only one die is recovered. Nothing can stop Wildeve now; he is possessed, perhaps just as he once let love possess him. When a moth extinguishes the lantern, Wildeve frantically gathers enough glowworms to produce light for the game. When he eventually loses all of the money, he sits stupefied, as Diggory disappears into the darkness.

Within moments, the newlyweds pass by in a carriage. Diggory stops them to ask about Thomasin. Learning that she is following soon, he waits until she rides up and, without explanation, hands her the money he's just won from her husband.

Unfortunately, this fine attempt to rectify an evil is marred by one mistake. Diggory thinks that the whole sum of 100 guineas belongs to Thomasin. This innocent error may cause more trouble than if the whole sum had been lost.

---

**NOTE: Good Intentions**   Mrs. Yeobright had thought she could do good by sending half the guineas to her son, but Christian's superstitiousness and Wildeve's deceit got in the way. Diggory tries to do good by winning back Thomasin's money, but his ignorance of the whole story gets in his way. It seems that chance ironically often causes decent actions to have evil results.

---

# BOOK FOUR: THE CLOSED DOOR

As we shall see, as simple a thing as a closed door will cause disaster for the major characters. People will misunderstand each other's motives, a marriage will founder, and one person will die. Again, it's the tiny details of chance that throw human lives into chaos. But perhaps that closed door can also be understood as a symbol for the past, which cannot be retrieved. Once events are set in motion, we can never stop fate.

# CHAPTER 1: THE RENCOUNTER BY THE POOL

It is July, and the heath glows in its one gorgeous season of the year. Similarly, Clym and Eustacia's marriage is glowing. They love everything because they are in love with each other. Such paradise cannot last, however, in Hardy's world. Clym finally returns to his studies, and Eustacia anxiously guesses that her hopes of moving soon to Paris are doomed.

Now, the misunderstandings over the guineas begin to multiply. Not having received a thank-you from Clym, Mrs. Yeobright begins to guess that Thomasin somehow received all one hundred guineas. Hearing that Eustacia is visiting Captain Vye, Clym's mother decides to ask her whether or not his share of the money ever arrived. Things are further complicated when Christian confesses that he lost all the money to Wildeve.

Notice how several small lies have built up into this confusion. Mrs. Yeobright didn't tell Wildeve about the money; he didn't tell Thomasin about the gambling incident; Thomasin promised Diggory she wouldn't tell her husband that she now has the money—these deceptions add up and cause great harm. And when Mrs. Yeobright rushes off to see Eustacia, she interprets Eustacia's evasive answers as evidence that Wildeve returned Clym's share to Eustacia, his former lover. Mrs. Yeobright suspects that Eustacia is cheating on Clym. Both women speak sharply, proudly, opening up old wounds. As they lash out at each other, we discover that each has been deeply hurt by the other and wants to get even. In her anger, Eustacia says that she wishes she hadn't married Clym, and predicts that the breach between Clym

and his mother will never be healed. Mrs. Yeobright
defends herself, warning Eustacia that if she ever
shows this kind of temper to Clym, she'll regret it.

Ironically, this encounter has taken place beside the
pond where Wildeve and Eustacia used to meet. As
her mother-in-law rushes off, Eustacia turns her gaze
toward the pool. Like us, she is surely reminded of
Wildeve by this symbol. Perhaps, she is thinking of
what might have been, if she had not driven him into
Thomasin's arms.

---

**NOTE: Anger as a Dangerous Passion**    During
this upsetting conversation, which woman was in the
wrong? If there is guilt, it is probably about equal.
Passion is still a dangerous force, even when it is
anger, not romantic love. This passion has made
Eustacia and Mrs. Yeobright deaf to each other, at
least for the moment, breeding more misunderstandings.

---

## CHAPTER 2: HE IS SET UPON BY
## ADVERSITIES; BUT HE SINGS A SONG

Clym notices Eustacia's emotional state when she
rushes home, and so she explains that his mother has
indirectly accused her of taking money from Wildeve.
Desperately, she suggests moving to Paris as an
answer to this galling situation. But he is astonished
that she thinks he would change his mind about Paris;
Eustacia glumly recognizes, all too well, that she has
been living in a dream. He will not discuss the issue,
and they turn away from each other—perhaps a fatal
first step.

The next day, the mystery of the money is cleared
up. Thomasin visits to give Clym his half. It is too late,

however, as Clym sadly realizes, to heal the quarrel between the two women who mean most to him.

More troubles lie in store for Clym. His concentrated studies bring on an acute inflammation of the eyes, making it impossible for him to read. As weeks pass, he does not improve, and Eustacia nervously fears that she will be chained to a lonely, boring existence, perhaps even with a blind husband.

Clym, on the other hand, remains cheerful. Walking out into the bright sun one day, he meets Humphrey, who is cutting furze. Though it is low-class work, Clym realizes that he could do it even in his present condition. As you'd expect, this decision horrifies Eustacia; it's just one more come-down in their status.

Clym ignores her objections, however. Daily, he works with Humphrey, finding peace and calm out in the fields. He almost merges with the heath; insects and small animals take his presence for granted.

Eustacia discovers Clym at work one morning happily singing a French love-song. Her pity for him turns in a flash to anger, the kind of anger that arises from despair. In the unsatisfactory conversation that follows, Clym realizes that her love for him has almost died; he says, however, he still loves her. She feels that she is the one who deserves pity, chained as she is to a life she despises. Clym tries gently to explain to her his philosophy about living humbly.

For all his fine ideas, however, Clym is missing the point. Independent, yearning Eustacia needs to see the greater life outside Egdon for herself. Dimly sighted Clym seems to be blind to this need. Consider what kind of schoolmaster Clym will make, if he expects his students to accept what he says without question. His conviction that he is right may be a kind of self-centeredness.

Rather than risk what her tongue might blurt out in response, Eustacia leaves him to his work. There is still affection between them; each is still trying to avoid directly attacking the other. As we're seeing, however, the gulf of misunderstanding between them is wide, and may be widening.

## CHAPTER 3: SHE GOES OUT TO BATTLE AGAINST DEPRESSION

It is late August. The brief shining summer of Egdon Heath is almost over, just as the brief shining marital happiness of Eustacia and Clym has dimmed. Clym optimistically expects the situation to improve, even though he realizes that, to his sobbing wife, he has changed from a hero into a common laborer.

Eustacia decides to fight off her deepening depression by going to East Egdon, where a village picnic will offer dancing. Clym's somewhat jealous, but he admits he would be a gloomy sight at such a festival and tells her to go on alone. Eustacia's spirit rebounds; she decides to hide her suffering from the world and act merry for an evening. Though you may not entirely admire Eustacia at this point, she does at least regain her former courage. When she dresses in a way that brightens her unusual beauty, even Hardy (who is often hard on her) comments that she might have good reason for resenting a life that doomed such charms to misery.

All is liveliness and young love at the East Egdon festivities. Unfortunately, Eustacia's female friend who had suggested the outing does not show up. Even independent-minded Eustacia cannot join in the dancing as a strange woman alone. But the sensuous, pagan spirit of the moonlit night enters Eustacia's blood, and she longs to join in the dancing. Suddenly, in this moment of frustrated emotions, Wildeve appears at her side.

It is their first encounter since his wedding day, and, by chance, it comes at a moment when Eustacia is very susceptible to Wildeve's appeal. Veiled, as if admitting that she's doing something improper, Eustacia accepts her former lover's invitation to dance. Soon, her pulse races. The dancing shows us her passionate nature, as she whirls and glides away from the boredom of her married life. Passion, once again, leads Eustacia astray.

The pair are united in pleasure, so obviously that the bystanders notice. As for Wildeve, this evening makes him once again want to have Eustacia as his own, all year long. When they sit down together on the grass to rest, Wildeve tenderly pries out the truth about Eustacia's unhappiness. He does seem more sympathetic in this scene—gentler, and more genuinely in love. Eustacia boldly accepts his offer to accompany her homeward, even though it would give the locals something to gossip about. The moonlight is bright, but the heath remains dark, and Eustacia needs Wildeve's touch to steady her from time to time. It's a delicate situation, and the danger must make it even more thrilling to them both.

Suddenly Clym appears, with Diggory, who is still Wildeve's determined adversary. In the dim light, Clym does not see Wildeve slip quietly away, from Eustacia but the reddleman does. After Clym and Eustacia head for home, he rushes to The Quiet Woman to catch Wildeve.

Thomasin tells Diggory that her husband has gone to East Egdon to buy a horse. Diggory, being surprisingly subtle, reports that he glimpsed her husband leading something home—"a beauty with a white face and a mane as black as night." Innocent Thomasin doesn't catch his reference, but we know he's talking about Eustacia. Wildeve, too, immediately understands the meaning of this comment when Thomasin reports it to him later. He realizes that Diggory is warning him, that he will be watching the reawakening of Wildeve's affair with Eustacia.

Diggory has also picked up a note of sadness beneath Thomasin's light tone when she jokes about husbands liking to play the truant. We can guess that the reddleman, who cares deeply about Thomasin's happiness, will be doing his best to prevent Wildeve from betraying her with Eustacia.

## CHAPTER 4: ROUGH COERCION IS EMPLOYED

Diggory's suspicions about Wildeve were aroused, it turns out, while he was just passing through the neighborhood. But now he is irresistibly drawn back into Thomasin's affairs. As he follows Wildeve, he realizes that so far Wildeve and Eustacia have not really taken up their old relationship again—yet. But Wildeve has taken up the suspicious habit of walking out at night to the Yeobright's cottage.

One night, as a warning, Diggory rigs up a trap that causes his enemy to stumble. Wildeve recognizes that the red-colored string in the trap is another warning from the persistent reddleman, but he continues his romantic walks, as if he had no power to stop. One night, he catches a moth and daringly slips it through the partly opened window of the Yeobright's cottage. The moth flies into a candle, and Eustacia recognizes the signal Wildeve used in the days of their love. Clym comes in and notices her agitation. She says she needs to go out for some air, but there is suddenly a loud knocking at the front door. When she answers it, no one is there, however. We learn that Diggory pounded on the door, so that Wildeve would have to sneak away. As he leaves the cottage, a gun is fired in his direction and he runs for cover, realizing that Venn may even want to hurt him seriously. Diggory's actions may seem odd, almost obsessive. He may also seem like a magical sprite here. Yet his tricks do not have quite the effect he intends. In fact, Wildeve realizes that it's too dangerous to visit Eustacia at night, and he decides to see her by day. Diggory's interference has hastened the affair, quite contrary to his desires.

Meanwhile, he continues his well-intended meddling by going to Mrs. Yeobright. He tells her that, in his view, both Clym and Thomasin would be happier if she would swallow her pride and visit them. Mrs. Yeobright pretends to remain firm, but Diggory's hints about Wildeve and Eustacia make her decide to visit her son; she has already decided to forgive him, anyway.

At the same moment, Clym is telling Eustacia that he wants to patch things up with his mother. He asks Eustacia to welcome his mother, if he is successful. Holding back her true feelings, she agrees not to interfere, but she refuses to go and make advances herself to Mrs. Yeobright.

---

**NOTE: The Consequences of an Action**    Repeatedly, Hardy sounds his theme that one action can be like a stone thrown into a pond and causing ever-widening circles to form. Clym's return has dramatically changed more lives than he knows. It is another form of blindness, perhaps, that keeps him, like all people, from realizing that his mistakes may have far-reaching consequences.

---

# CHAPTER 5: THE JOURNEY ACROSS THE HEATH

On an oppressively hot day, the last day of August, Mrs. Yeobright walks across the heath to make up with Clym and Eustacia. The air, says Hardy, is like the inside of a kiln, a furnace for firing pottery. Mrs. Yeobright feels the strain and must rest frequently. Because she has never visited her son's cottage, she further tires herself by taking wrong pathways, all of them uphill.

Coming upon a laborer, she asks the way. The man simply tells her to follow an anonymous furze-cutter, walking in the distance, Mrs. Yeobright slowly realizes that the unknown furze-cutter is Clym. The revelation disturbs her so much that she instantly begins scheming to rescue him and Eustacia. Ironically, her wishes are for once the same as those of her dissatisfied daughter-in-law.

From a distance, she sees Clym enter his cottage. Tired and emotionally upset, she sits down to rest a moment on a hill. The broken, scarred trees around her produce a mysterious foreboding moan. As she sits there, Mrs. Yeobright spies a man circling Clym's cottage below, then going in. She's annoyed, at first but then she decides that this stranger's arrival might be a good thing after all; it could make her entrance easier, since everyone would be forced to be casual and polite.

The chapter ends with a masterful picture of a hot, lazy summer afternoon—a sleeping housecat, metallically glaring leaves, wasps rolling on the ground drunk with apple juice. This quiet moment will prove to be the calm before the storm. Mrs. Yeobright is last seen at Clym's garden gate, poised to begin her attempt at making peace.

# CHAPTER 6: A CONJUNCTURE, AND ITS RESULT UPON THE PEDESTRIAN

Hardy now backs up to explain why another person has appeared at Clym and Eustacia's cottage this afternoon. Wildeve, again bewitched by Eustacia's spell, cannot resist seeing her. So as not to compromise her, he has decided to visit her openly, even when Clym might be at home.

When Wildeve enters, Eustacia gives him a cool reception. She shows him Clym, who has fallen asleep on a rug on the floor. Eustacia certainly sees the contrast between her dirty, weary husband and the buoyant, well-dressed Wildeve, but she is not ready to throw over Clym. She admits to Wildeve that the marriage is not working, but blames Clym's eye trouble. Wildeve makes it clear that he still loves her; she admits that she's not exactly unhappy to hear that, considering the state of her marriage. Moved by feelings they cannot express, they gaze enviously at the sleeping Clym, who seems to possess a sense of peace which neither of them can achieve.

They are startled by a knock on the door. Mrs. Yeobright is there, about to walk in on a scene which would confirm all her suspicions of Eustacia. Fate, seems once again to have dealt Eustacia an unfair blow. Her reactions whirl—she wants to hide Wildeve; she longs to be seen with him, no matter what her mother-in-law might think; she's unwilling to open the door to a woman who dislikes her so much.

When the knocking is repeated, Clym mumbles the word, "Mother," in his sleep. Eustacia's certain that he will answer the knock, and now it's more important that Wildeve must not be seen. Eustacia slips with her former lover out the back door, telling him quite firmly never to visit again. She waits by herself in the garden—partly because she might be in the way, partly because she is not eager to face Mrs. Yeobright. Throughout this scene, her emotions have been mixed, confused, contradictory.

Soon, Eustacia notices that the cottage is silent. Going in, she discovers that Clym never woke up. She rushes to open the door, but it is too late; there's no one there, nothing but the great hot silent heath.

Out of sight, Mrs. Yeobright is struggling homeward. She's half-mad with distress, because she glimpsed Eustacia's face through a window and, knowing that Clym was inside, she assumes that he willingly allowed his wife to keep the door barred against his mother.

By chance, little Johnny Nunsuch idly appears on the path beside Mrs. Yeobright. As she rambles on about Eustacia's coldheartedness and Clym's rejection, the boy tells her she is talking nonsense. As he describes how she looks to him—pale, sweating, and almost in convulsions—we suspect that there's more than a little weariness affecting her.

She finally sits down, scarcely able to breathe, and pulls out a small teacup, ironically one of a set which she was going to give as a peace offering to Clym and Eustacia. Johnny brings her some lukewarm pond water, but it is too nauseating to drink. Bored, the boy asks to leave, but Mrs. Yeobright sends him off with a dreadful messsage, ". . . you have seen a broken-hearted woman cast off by her son."

Alone, exposed to the draining sun, this once-proud, independent woman creeps along feebly.

Hardy, in this chapter, has been almost as hard on the reader as Fate has been on the characters. Helpless, we watch people make decisions which bring on disaster. It's frustrating to know what Mrs. Yeobright cannot—that her son loves her, that Eustacia did not mean for her to be shut out.

Why did Wildeve have to visit the cottage at that particular moment? Why didn't Clym wake up fully? Why did Mrs. Yeobright happen to see Eustacia in the window? These tiny tricks of fate seem to lead to cruel consequences.

Is Eustacia to blame for slipping away? Is Mrs. Yeobright to blame, because she was so stubborn in the beginning? As we have seen before, Hardy does not give simple answers to these questions. He wants his novel to be as puzzling as life itself is.

---

**NOTE: Frustrating Fate**    Often, Hardy's readers are shown that unfortunate happenings could be avoided "if only" some small thing had happened otherwise. If this makes you feel frustrated, it is just what the novelist wants you to feel. He does not believe we can control our lives.

---

## CHAPTER 7: THE TRAGIC MEETING OF TWO OLD FRIENDS

Back at the cottage, Clym wakes up from a terrible dream. In it, Eustacia and he went to visit his mother, but could not get in, even though she was heard screaming for help. This dream—so close to the truth, if he only knew it!—makes him wonder why his mother still hasn't broken her silence. He decides to break down and go visit her this evening. When she hears this, Eustacia offers to go to Blooms-End herself. She hopes, of course, to apologize to Mrs. Yeobright, and clear up the whole matter before Clym can even hear about it. But Clym, puzzled, insists on going himself. Both, in different ways, want to take action, without knowing that it is already too late.

At sunset, Clym walks off on the darkened heath for several miles. Scenting his mother's perfume (how well he knows her!) he stops, and a faint moan reaches his ears. He discovers with shock his mother, lying in a heap at his feet. He carries her limp body toward Blooms-End, but decides he'd better stop and set her down in a small shed about a mile from her cottage. Making her as comfortable as possible on a bed of dried fern, he runs off to get help.

Soon, the country folk arrive. They discover that she has been bitten by an adder, or snake. Sam suggests an old folk remedy—frying other adders to produce fat for an ointment. Two freshly killed snakes, and one live one, are found. Mrs. Yeobright and the living snake stare at each other; it looks angry and evil, causing her to tremble. The country folk, too, see evil in the snake. Yet, while the remedy is being prepared, they chatter on, their familiar characters as unchanging, in their way, as Egdon Heath. Susan Nunsuch, Johnny's mother, brings a frying-pan, and the snakes are cooked. Clym, the man of progressive ideas, finds himself gently anointing his mother's wound with this crude ointment, if only because the doctor has not yet arrived.

Here is the reconciliation that both mother and son have desired for so long. But it's scarcely satisfying; She is barely conscious and may be dying; he doesn't know if he has been forgiven; she may not even be aware of his tender nursing. A cruel price has been paid for this reunion.

---

NOTE:   Mrs. Yeobright's Death as a Public Event
Notice that Hardy purposely turns this scene into a public event. Just as at the bonfire and at the Christ-

mas party, the villagers have gathered to comment and observe, and thus we are reminded of the social context of the Yeobright's private tragedy. Ironically, the villagers may feel more comfortable with Mrs. Yeobright, who thinks herself superior, than with her son, who wants so badly to educate them. If she dies, it will be an event of major importance to the Egdon area. One generation will have passed on, leaving room for the new. If she dies, some of the values of the past may also die.

---

## CHAPTER 8: EUSTACIA HEARS OF GOOD FORTUNE AND BEHOLDS EVIL

Alone at home, Eustacia is depressed, fearing there will be some ugly consequences of her not opening the door. Yet she doesn't blame herself, but Providence.

Deciding to walk out to meet Clym on his way homeward, she instead encounters Captain Vye. He reports that Wildeve has unexpectedly inherited a huge fortune from an uncle in Canada. Eustacia's grandfather calls her a fool for not hanging on to him, she wonders why Wildeve didn't tell her this news when he came to visit.

As she reflects, Wildeve himself re-appears. Casually, they walk together to meet Clym. When she asks him about the inheritance, he gallantly says he hadn't told her because her own fortunes were not so happy. She changes the subject and Wildeve explains his plans to invest most of the money and use the rest for a year's travel to the world's most exciting places—beginning, of course, with Paris. Without knowing of Eustacia's dreams of Paris, he too yearns toward it. These two people resemble each other, even in their longings. They begin to talk over the past; Wildeve hints that he would never have married Thomasin if Eustacia hadn't rejected him.

Suddenly, they see a light ahead, cast by the shed where Mrs. Yeobright lies. Hidden in the dark, they overhear the doctor tell Clym that his mother's in danger, not so much from the bite as from exhaustion. She is sinking fast. We hear Mrs. Yeobright's last gasp. Then little Johnny Nunsuch shrieks out her words to him: "she said I was to say that I had seed her, and she was a broken-hearted woman and cast off by her son." Clym sobs miserably. Eustacia, concealed in darkness (as we've seen her so often), is torn between comforting him and avoiding exposure.

Deciding to slip away, Eustacia faces putting the blame on herself at last. She tells Wildeve that she cannot speak to him any more. As he vanishes, she can see only one sight—the procession carrying the body of her mother-in-law. Figuratively, too, she sees only this because it is now the most important fact in her life. Book Four, titled "The Closed Door," concludes with the most terrible consequence of Eustacia's neglecting to open that door: Mrs. Yeobright's death.

# BOOK FIVE:
# THE DISCOVERY

By now, you can guess the meaning of Hardy's title. It seems likely that Eustacia's act will be discovered. Notice that Hardy often uses titles that give away what will happen. Perhaps he is less interested in surprising us with developments of plot than with reminding us of his themes. He wants us to think about what happens to Eustacia and whether or not she deserves her fate. He wants us to study, along with him, how tragedy can occur when ordinary people try to live fulfilling lives.

## CHAPTER 1: "WHEREFORE IS LIGHT GIVEN TO HIM THAT IS IN MISERY?"

Weeks later, in the moonlight outside their cottage, we see Eustacia, who has been faithfully nursing the grief-torn Clym. When Humphrey stops by, she tells him that her husband's delirium has subsided, but he is still obsessed by thoughts of his mother. Eustacia goes back inside, where Clym twists and turns, accusing himself of causing Mrs. Yeobright's death. He says hopelessly, "If she had only come to see me!" Obviously, then, Eustacia still hasn't told him about the aborted visit. As Clym wails in despair and guilt, his wife is again and again reminded of her own guilt.

Thomasin arrives, hoping to comfort Clym, but he rises to new heights of grief. Eustacia holds her tongue, but Clym rages on, condemning himself, wildly picturing his mother dying, Eustacia feels even more guilty. When he calls on God to punish him, she knows that it is she who deserves punishment.

Thomasin gently urges her cousin to calm down. We learn that she is about to have a child; afterwards, she and Wildeve mean to begin their travels.

---

NOTE: **Life Goes On** As we have seen throughout the novel, Hardy believes in the continuity of life itself at Egdon, no matter what happens to individuals. Mrs. Yeobright has died, but, as if to restore the natural balance, a new soul is about to enter the world. Wildeve's plans for a new lifestyle are being carried out, even though Eustacia's life has sunk into a dull round of duty.

---

For Clym, life has stopped. Reverting to his own concerns, he again repeats his mother's accusing last message; tortured, Eustacia begs him to stop. Thomasin, level-headed, reminds Clym that his mother often spoke in haste, and she'd probably forgiven him, nonetheless.

Wildeve drives up outside, and Eustacia goes out to tell him that Thomasin is coming in a few minutes. Wretchedly, she confesses that she has not yet told Clym the story of the closed door. She wants to tell him, but she's afraid that, in his present state, Clym might actually kill her. His overmastering grief, we see, is another example of the sort of passion that can destroy reason. Wildeve, typically the diplomat, suggests that Eustacia not confess until Clym is better; even then, she shouldn't reveal that Wildeve himself was on the scene that day. Eustacia, ever the pragmatic one, agrees.

When Thomasin and Wildeve drive off together, their shared future looks bright, with the promise of a child and exciting travel. Eustacia watches them sadly; her own future looks dark indeed.

## CHAPTER 2: A LURID LIGHT BREAKS IN UPON A DARKENED UNDERSTANDING

Clym improves over the following month, if only because his grief wears out. Now, however he is unnaturally silent.

While Clym is working in the garden one evening, Eustacia brings the happy news that Thomasin has given birth to a baby girl. As you may suspect, however, simple-minded Christian also brings trouble, as he has so often before. He reports that he saw Mrs. Yeobright the day she died, setting out on the six-mile walk to Clym's place. Christian doesn't know why she was coming, but he suggests that Diggory, who has been away lately, might. This news, which might have comforted Clym, has come too late. If Christian weren't so addle-brained, and if Venn had not vanished, Clym might not have had to suffer his long ordeal of terrible remorse.

In any event, Clym sets off one day to Blooms-End because the property is now his legal responsibility. As he wanders through his childhood home, he looks fondly on the old family furnishings, which he knows Eustacia would want to get rid of. Great differences still exist between husband and wife.

Coincidentally, Venn appears at the cottage; he's shocked when he learns that Mrs. Yeobright is dead. The two men sit down in the large room where, only the previous Christmas, life had seemed so carefree. Change is one of Hardy's themes: change which brings the death of hopes, the death of people.

Diggory, we learn, spoke with Mrs. Yeobright the night before she died. He tells Clym that she didn't blame him at all. This news does not satisfy Clym. He wants to know what could have changed her mind, to make her give her bitter message to Johnny Nunsuch.

When Diggory leaves, the puzzle continues to eat away at Clym. After a sleepless night at Blooms-End, he decides to question Johnny again. The next morning he takes the path to the Nunsuch cottage, feeling a chill in the air—a possible bad omen.

When Susan answers Clym's knock, he recalls how she pricked Eustacia with a needle. In fact, Johnny is ill again, and his mother believes Eustacia is to blame.

In a sense, she has her revenge on Eustacia now. Her son Johnny reveals to the astonished Clym that he saw the whole episode: Mrs. Yeobright resting at the Devil's Bellows, a gentleman entering Clym's cottage, Mrs. Yeobright knocking at the door, Eustacia watching her from a window.

Wildly, Clym ricochets from bewilderment to anger, finally shouting, "May all murderesses get the torment they deserve!" He doesn't have to use Eustacia's name; we know whom he means. Clym seems possessed by a mood in which anything is possible.

---

**NOTE: Mankind's Insignificance** Distraught and dangerous as Clym becomes, the face of the heath in contrast is "imperturbable." Just as the action heats up to fever pitch, the novelist reminds us that a single man's tragedy means nothing to this ancient wasteland. Probably, he is suggesting that all of mankind's troubles and joys are insignificant, when compared with the long existence of the earth. What we most fear or love is forgotten in time. Mankind is probably not the center of the universe. The universe probably pays no attention to us.

---

## CHAPTER 3: EUSTACIA DRESSES HERSELF ON A BLACK MORNING

Clym rushes home in a fury. When he enters Eustacia's room, she has just woken up and is seated at her mirror. In the glass, she sees his face, which is "ashy, haggard, and terrible." With a frightening kind of intimacy, the pallor of his face tranfers immediately to his wife's. Instantly, each understands the other.

Eustacia, however, plays for time. She pretends not to understand his hints about Wildeve's visit; exasperated, Clym says that he's referring to the day Eustacia "shut the door against my mother and killed her." Coolly she asks if he means to kill her, but he answers no, for that would make a martyr of her; besides, death might cause her to meet Mrs. Yeobright in the after-life, and Clym wants them kept apart eternally. Matching his desperation with her own, Eustacia says she almost wishes he would kill her, since their marriage is such a disaster.

Clym will not be distracted, however; he wants to know what happened when his mother tried to visit. In her defiance, Eustacia refuses to explain. Clym breaks into her writing desk and finds, among her private letters, a single empty envelope addressed to Eustacia in Wildeve's handwriting.

In the wild scene that follows, Clym virtually accuses his wife of adultery; in revenge, she allows him to be tortured by his suspicions. Bitter remarks and recriminations flash back and forth.

Then, suddenly, Eustacia begins to cry and, trembling, offers her hand to her husband. We must remember how precious this hand is to Charley, how precious it has been to Clym. Reluctantly, he takes it, but he says he's been bewitched by her—in the past. Eustacia falls to her knees, begging for pity. Clym refuses until she names the man who was in the house with her. She will not. They remain at an impasse. They even disagree over which of them should move out. Eustacia finally decides to leave. In one of Hardy's most dramatically poignant moments, Clym, seeing that the woman who once fascinated him is too upset to tie her own bonnet, gently ties it for her. But his parting words are unyielding; Eustacia leaves without answering him.

Soon afterward, word comes to Clym that the Wild-eves have named their baby girl "Eustacia Clementine." This is a cruel joke, in his eyes. The girl's two names will honor a marriage that has turned cold and hollow.

# CHAPTER 4: THE MINISTRATIONS OF A HALF-FORGOTTEN ONE

After showing Clym's uncontrollable anger—the passionate result of his pain and loss—Hardy concentrates now on Eustacia's misery. Again and again, he reminds us of the contrast between her present state and her earlier hopes. She wanders through "the dying ferns" which were so luxuriant when she and Clym decided to marry. Reaching her grandfather's cottage, which had always been her home, she finds it locked and empty. Charley is there, however, and he is stunned to see her desperate state. Previously, she only let him touch her as part of a deal; now, she leans on him for physical support. He opens up the house, lights a fire, and helps her eat and drink a little. Even his kindness reminds her of better times.

After lying on a couch lifelessly for a while, Eustacia goes upstairs to her old room. It hasn't changed, a fact which harshly reminds her of her own changed situation. Hardy stresses that it is autumn, the season of dying things. His heroine spies a pair of pistols in her grandfather's room. She quickly goes downstairs and considers committing suicide.

When she finally resolves to kill herself, however, and returns upstairs for the weapons, they are gone. Charley is standing outside; Eustacia realizes that the shy, uneducated boy has guessed her intentions. She asks him for the pistols, which he has locked up in the stable, but he refuses, because he loves Eustacia too much to let her kill herself. At this moment, when Eustacia has been feeling completely alone in the world, Charley's love revives her. He promises not to tell what has happened; she promises that the moment has passed.

That night, her grandfather kindly asks no questions when he sees her emotional state. Eustacia tells him only that she will stay again with him.

---

**NOTE: Simple People's Humanity**      Note that the simple people whom Eustacia spurned, such as Charley and her grandfather, show sincere human feeling to her now, while the sophisticated Wildeve, the idealistic Clym, are not there when Eustacia hits rock bottom. Many readers feel that Hardy is saying here that human decency and generosity are more likely to be found among simple folk than in a cosmopolitan setting. Eustacia, as we have seen, does not appreciate such virtues as much as she might; this has hastened her downfall. Hardy may want us to see that her inability to enjoy and understand the humble people of Egdon is a great failing.

---

At this point, Eustacia is probably thinking only of herself and of her ruined hopes. Love has died, her marriage has ended, and she may never see Paris. She has returned to the center of the heath that she despises.

## CHAPTER 5: AN OLD MOVE INADVERTENTLY REPEATED

For days, Eustacia remains lifeless. Charley, happy to be her guardian, does every little thing he can to give her pleasure.

Eventually, she returns to her old habit of looking through her grandfather's telescope. In the past, she might have been searching eagerly for her lover, Wildeve. Now, by contrast, she sees her own furniture being moved by Clym to his mother's house. Rather than see promise, she watches a defeat. On another day, she sees Thomasin out walking, the baby in her arms, as a nursemaid follows. Eustacia's lonely, abandoned life contrasts with her old rival's maternal happiness.

Meanwhile, Charley has been preparing for November 5, expecting that Eustacia will want a good bonfire again as she did in the past. He does not know, of course, that for those two years, the bonfire was a signal to Wildeve. On the evening of Guy Fawkes Day, exactly one year after the beginning of this novel, Charley kindles the fire, even though Eustacia is inside the cottage, with the shutters closed.

Charley's good, if mistaken, intentions, set the plot going again, as if he is an unknowing agent of fate. On first seeing the fire blaze up, Eustacia asks Charley to put it out. She does not want to see Wildeve—or does she? She doesn't insist very hard, as Charley lets the fire blaze on. She seems numbed, willing to take whatever happens.

Skillfully, the novelist unnerves Eustacia, and perhaps us too, with that sound we know so well—the splash of a stone in the pond. Eustacia, shocked, cannot move. Wildeve, still unseen, throws a second stone. She moves toward him.

In the firelight, separated by the earth-bank, they speak directly, urgently, with the familiarity of former lovers. Eustacia urges him to stay back; as though she's concealing herself; Wildeve, nevertheless, can see how unhappy she is. Eustacia, once so aggressive, almost mannish, and resilient, now breaks down in sobs. Wildeve offers to do anything he can to save her. He seems more under her power than he's ever been. She asks help to get secretly to Budmouth, from where she can travel at last to Paris. She seems unable to speak when he asks if he can go with her.

Perhaps she still feels bound by decency to her marriage; perhaps, after all, she still loves Clym. Perhaps she is simply not sure about Wildeve. Hardy doesn't tell us, possibly because Eustacia herself doesn't know. She knows she can use Wildeve "as a friend" or, more irrevocably, she can become his lover. She puts off this decision until later; if she does decide to let him come along, she tells him, he'll see a signal some night at eight o'clock. Then they can leave together at midnight that same night.

The chapter ends in confusion—Eustacia rushing away in a frenzy, Wildeve staring from the darkness as she disappears. Charley's bonfire, lit to divert her from her depression, has led her toward taking a step she had not considered before. Charley may have saved Eustacia from killing herself, but now, unwittingly, he's brought her into another kind of danger. Can Eustacia escape her imprisonment on Egdon Heath? Can we ever escape our own particular fates? That is the question Hardy poses now.

## CHAPTER 6: THOMASIN ARGUES WITH HER COUSIN, AND HE WRITES A LETTER

Meanwhile, Clym is already hoping that Eustacia will come back to him. As he cleans up his mother's house, the slightest sound causes him to think his wife has reappeared. Notice that, even though his anger has cooled, he still expects her to make the first move; Clym still can't admit he was wrong.

His suspicions about Wildeve have not weakened, but on November 5, the night of Charley's bonfire, in frustration Clym decides to visit The Quiet Woman, hoping that Wildeve will say something that might clear Eustacia's honor. By chance, Wildeve has already gone off (to Eustacia's cottage, we know) when Clym arrives. Clym talks to Thomasin about his marital difficulties, though he tactfully does not mention that Wildeve may be involved. Thomasin is horrified nevertheless. Always the peacemaker, she urges Clym to send for Eustacia and patch things up. Remember, it was also Thomasin who wanted peace between Clym and his mother. Gentle Thomasin, who has suffered much, does not want others to suffer.

Clym agrees to take her advice. That night at Blooms-End, he writes a rambling but heartfelt plea to Eustacia. He promises not to mention the past, if Eustacia will only return. Yet he puts the letter aside for a day, still hoping she will come back first. This decision, surely an act of pride, will turn out to be disastrous.

Meanwhile, Wildeve has come back home, where Thomasin waits with anxiety. She has noticed his recent gloominess, his feeling that Egdon Heath is a jail. She complains that he never takes her on his frequent walks. In fact, she confesses, she followed him this evening and heard him say, "Damn it, I'll go!" before vanishing into the darkness. Wildeve is angry at her for this, but when she begins to cry, explaining that she has heard rumors about him and Eustacia, Wildeve calms down. He does not like scenes, and neither does Thomasin. But though Wildeve prevents a quarrel, to avoid any messy emotional scenes, he obviously still has no intention of behaving as Thomasin would like him to. In fact, her fears may even make him realize that he must act soon, if he wants Eustacia. We can only guess, of course, for the Wildeves are happy to leave many things unsaid.

## CHAPTER 7: THE NIGHT OF THE SIXTH OF NOVEMBER

The next day, Eustacia is eager to leave Egdon. Clym could still change her mind, but he does not appear. Toward late afternoon, she packs a small bundle, as an ominous storm begins to rise upon the heath's horizon.

At eight, Eustacia signals Wildeve with a burning branch. An answering light appears instantly beside The Quiet Woman; Wildeve has been watching vigilantly. The plan is therefore set in motion—they will meet at midnight.

After supper, Eustacia goes to her bedroom to rest, while Captain Vye sits up, drinking alone. At about ten, Fairway appears, bearing Clym's letter to Eustacia. Ironically, he had the letter for a while, but he forgot it until now. If he had remembered earlier, Eustacia might have still been downstairs. As it is, Captain Vye assume she's asleep and puts the letter on the mantelpiece, for her to see the next day. Hardy draws out the suspense hovering over this undelivered letter. Much later, as Captain Vye prepares for bed, he notices a light in her room, and later he hears her crying as she passes his door. He goes out into the hall to tell her about the letter, but it is too late. She has disappeared.

Alarmed, Vye discovers that the front door is unlocked. The letter still sits on the mantel, untouched; we realize that Eustacia has gone off without knowing that Clym wanted her back. Is it just a cruel coincidence? Hardy points out that her determination to leave is now so strong that even the letter really would not have stopped her. Neither does the bad weather, or the night, which has become black and heavy, making us think of death, or the dark forces of fate.

Alone at Rainbarrow, where we first met her, Eustacia stands storm-tossed, without and within. Questions whirl in her brain. What will she do for money? Will she have to humiliate herself by becoming Wildeve's mistress? Notice that she still has her pride and moral standards intact; mere passion would not drive her into his arms. She sobs aloud and talks wildly, saying that Wildeve is "not *great* enough" to satisfy her longings, or to cause her to break the vow of marriage. Yet, she has no money. In a frenzy, she blames fate, "things beyond [her] control" for ruining her life.

Suddenly, Hardy pulls back from the passion of this desperate scene to show Susan Nunsuch, warm and secure in her cottage. In strangely fascinating detail, he describes her making a small doll out of melted beeswax and giving it Eustacia's features. Believing in old superstitions, she is making a sort of voodoo doll. First, she sticks pins into the wax figure. Then she holds it over her fire with tongs, murmuring the Lord's Prayer backwards as the doll melts.

---

NOTE: The Magical Doll   When Susan works her spell, we remember the many times that Eustacia has been associated with fire—and with fiery passion. Hardy may not be asking us to believe that the spell works in a literal way, but, just as the image is consumed by fire, so, is Eustacia consumed by the fire of her passions. And, just as the image is destroyed by superstitious Susan, Eustacia has probably been de-

stroyed in part by the ignorance and superstition
which have surrounded and suffocated her at Egdon.

---

# CHAPTER 8: RAIN, DARKNESS, AND ANXIOUS WANDERERS

As the storm gets worse, Clym anxiously waits at
Blooms-End, hoping for a reply to his letter—maybe
even a visit from Eustacia herself. He nonetheless falls
asleep, only to be aroused by a female voice. Eagerly,
he opens the door, thinking Eustacia has returned,
but it is instead Thomasin, looking pitiful, with her
baby in her arms. She reports that Wildeve means to
run off with Eustacia, but he hasn't left yet; she wants
Clym to persuade him not to go. He agrees.

As Clym is dressing, Captain Vye appears next,
looking for Eustacia. He has just heard from Charley
about the incident with the pistols, and fears that
Eustacia has gone off to kill herself. Clym assures him
they will find her at Wildeve's, but Vye decides to
return home to wait for her. Clym heads for The Quiet
Woman.

For some time, Thomasin tries to wait patiently. But
unable to endure the suspense, she finally snatches
up her daughter and plunges back into the pouring
rain. Her journey is difficult, but her reaction to the
wild weather is, unlike Eustacia's, accepting and rational. Despite her familiarity with the heath, though,
she eventually gets lost, and, coincidentally, she
comes upon Diggory Venn's empty van.

Suddenly, as if by magic, he appears. In the confusion of the stormy night, he doesn't recognize Thomasin at first. In fact, he says, some other woman had

just passed by, sobbing; Thomasin intuitively knows it must have been Eustacia, and resolves to find her. Diggory takes the baby carefully, following Thomasin's firm, brusque instructions. Notice that she seems much stronger with this man than with her husband.

When they see a light, she thinks they've reached the inn, but Diggory stops her from heading on alone, and saves her from falling into a deep swamp. Once again, Venn has protected Thomasin from danger. Even so, she will not trust him with the secret of what is going on. Perhaps she simply is too loyal, or too proud, to tell a man who loves her that her husband is about to run away.

## CHAPTER 9: SIGHTS AND SOUNDS DRAW THE WANDERERS TOGETHER

Notice the purposely deadpan tone of this chapter title. Suspense is high, but Hardy pretends that events are happening by themselves, that even he is not in control.

As we now learn, Wildeve had decided that money would solve everything. He planned to ease his conscience by leaving half his inheritance to Thomasin; then Eustacia could share the rest with him. Hardy, however, probably would not agree that money by itself is the answer to any human problem; Wildeve is shallow and deluded. He is also being stood up. He waits in the rain with his horse and gig until a quarter past midnight. At the sound of a footstep, he rushes forward, calling "Eustacia?"; the light from his lamp falls upon Clym. Hardy seems to be stressing that the unexpected is part of life. Wildeve awaits his love; instead, he finds her husband.

Suddenly, the two men are startled by the sound of a body falling into the nearby stream near a weir, or small dam. Clym immediately senses it must be Eustacia, alarming Wildeve.

Together, the rivals rush to the circular pool below the weir. Swollen by the storm, it has become a raging whirlpool. They glimpse a body in the water; Wildeve jumps in passionately, without thinking. Typically, Clym acts more rationally, first positioning the lamp and then wading in from a shallow area. Nonetheless, he too is drawn into the whirlpool.

Now Thomasin and Diggory arrive on the scene. Venn, hands the baby to Thomasin and tells her to rush home for help. Notice the symbolism behind the actions of each character in this scene: just as in their emotional lives, Wildeve is impulsive, Clym tries to be calm but is swept away, and Diggory plods through competently to the end.

Finally, Diggory seizes a body and drags it out. It is a man, with another man clutching onto his legs. As help arrives, the unconscious figures are laid upon the grass. It was Wildeve, holding on to Clym. Some readers think Wildeve grabbed Clym to save himself; others think he was trying to drag Clym down with him. Your answer will depend on your final assessment of Wildeve's character.

Quickly, the pool is probed with a pole, and an object is felt. Again, Venn goes into the water, and comes up with Eustacia's cold body.

The three victims are taken back to The Quiet Woman and laid close to the fire. Eventually, Clym alone comes back to life. Diggory, uncertain of the role he should play now, leaves and then wanders back. Thomasin has thoughtfully left a message that Diggory should have whatever he wants. He stands by the fireplace, pondering how things have changed since the raffle, the last time he was there. Like Hardy, Diggory sees the future is uncertain, appearances can deceive, and there is no such thing in human affairs as permanence. The nurse comes downstairs, to try to dry out the paper money found on Wildeve's body, but we realize that all his lucky money can't help him now.

Early in the morning, Charley appears for news of Eustacia. Looking dead himself, Clym allows Charley to view her corpse. Ironically, both Eustacia and Wildeve look as handsome as ever in death, although Wildeve's fingers show telling scars of a desperate failed attempt to hold on to life.

The atmosphere of peace is shattered, however, by Clym's eerie remark, that Eustacia is the second woman he's killed this year. Diggory tells him not to feel responsible, but Clym cannot listen. No matter how good his intentions were, the consequences have been tragic. He feels that no punishment will ever help him atone for being involved in the deaths of two women he loved.

Was Clym really at fault? Or was he the victim of chance occurrences? Could both things be true at once? Hardy lets you wrestle with that problem on your own.

# BOOK SIX: AFTERCOURSES

Because of public demand, Hardy changed his intended ending in this short, final book. Readers who had been following this tale of Egdon Heath in magazine form, as it first appeared, did not want to be left with a completely unhappy conclusion. Against his original plan, Hardy now lets some light and joy into this novel of darkness and tragedy.

# CHAPTER 1: THE INEVITABLE MOVEMENT ONWARD

Their death makes Eustacia and Wildeve become legendary in the Egdon area, as if these two had really been larger than life. Yet Thomasin's private grief for her husband is gradually eased over the following year, by the delight of seeing baby Eustacia grow. Thomasin and her daughter move back to Blooms-End, where Clym keeps to himself in a couple of upstairs rooms. Thomasin is now wealthy and independent, with Wildeve's legacy, but she and her cousin live quite simply.

Unlike Eustacia, Clym does not blame fate for his situation; he bitterly reproaches himself. As another year passes, Clym is still only dimly aware of the happy domestic life shared by Thomasin and her daughter in their part of the house. He is studying again, using books with very large type because of his still-weak vision. Clym seems scarred, crippled almost by his tragedy.

One summer day, Diggory appears at Blooms-End. He's a new man, no longer stained with red. As Clym enters, Venn explains that he's given up the reddleman's trade to take over his late father's dairy herd. He and Thomasin are uneasy with each other, but Clym, typically, does not notice.

We learn that the common folk are going to put up a Maypole in an adjacent field for a festival the following day. That evening, Clym watches as the young people wreathe the pole with wildflowers.

**NOTE: The Symbol of the Maypole**     The Maypole, Hardy notes, is a relic of pagan customs.
Remember that we have already seen festivals associated with other seasons: the Christmas party in
winter, the moonlight dance in summer, the bonfires
of autumn. Now we will see the festival of spring,
symbolic of fertility and renewed life. It suggests that
new life may also be possible for Thomasin.

---

The next morning, Thomasin wakes to see the pole
in place and smell the sweet fragrance of its flowers.
The sight delights her, and, for the first time since
Wildeve's death, she dresses in bright clothes. Clym
compliments her. When she blushes, he suddenly
wonders if she might be trying to attract him. It's an
unsettling thought; love, for him, burnt itself out with
Eustacia. As the brass band arrives, Clym slips away,
unable to endure the good times. He doesn't return
until dusk, when the scene is quiet again. Thomasin,
he learns, had not joined the party, out of a sense of
propriety.

Outside, one figure remains, strolling idly; it is Diggory. Thomasin tells him that she watched him dance
and noticed that he had his pick of dancing partners
all evening. Venn says he is waiting for the moon to
rise so that he can find a glove dropped by an
unnamed young woman, someone he did not dance
with. Thomasin is astounded, particularly since he
still has a long walk home ahead of him.

From inside the house, she watches as he searches.
She tells herself that she is annoyed that he should
behave so foolishly, now that he's respectable, but we
may detect an undercurrent of jealousy. Finally, she
sees Diggory find the glove and kiss it before putting it
in his breast-pocket.

## CHAPTER 2: THOMASIN WALKS IN A GREEN PLACE BY THE ROMAN ROAD

Days later, Thomasin tells Clym that she is still wondering about the identity of the owner of the glove, fretting that none of the dancers was good enough for Diggory. Thomasin's gentle, childish obsession is a touching sign of her awakening emotions—far different from the wild passions we've seen other lovers show.

Some time later, Thomasin cannot find one of her own gloves. Rachel, a young servant, confesses that she borrowed Thomasin's gloves for the Maypole dance and lost one. Diggory, Rachel adds, knew this. Stunned, Thomasin ponders this information all afternoon.

The next day, Diggory appears on horseback as Thomasin is playing with little Eustacia on the heath. Thomasin abruptly asks for the glove. Diggory pulls it out of his breast-pocket. As they go on talking they begin to tease each other, beginning a flirtation. Soon, the two are meeting regularly at this hollow of the heath, near the old Roman road. A new cycle of love begins in this ancient, timeless place.

## CHAPTER 3: THE SERIOUS DISCOURSE OF CLYM WITH HIS COUSIN

Meanwhile, ironically, Clym has begun to feel that it may be his duty to marry Thomasin. He feels he does not love her, but he feels sorry for her, and, after all, his mother, always wanted them to get together. Some readers think Clym is fooling himself, talking himself into doing something he really wants to do anyway. Others feel he's being honest when he admits he is "a mere corpse of a lover."

Finally, Clym decides to let Thomasin decide. When he tries to bring up the subject with her, however, she has news of her own; she wants his approval of her decision to marry. Once more, Clym's indecision has made him delay an action until it's too late. He gives her his approval—until he learns that her choice is Venn. Clym, for all his idealistic love of his fellow man, secretly shares his mother's strain of snobbery, and he doesn't think Diggory is good enough. But Thomasin knows herself; she admits that she has "countrified ways," and says she "couldn't be happy anywhere else but Egdon." (How unlike Eustacia!)

To do him credit, Clym doesn't really want to be an obstacle; he appreciates Venn's honest, kind, steady qualities. Thomasin points out that Diggory is much more respectable in his new line of work. Some days later, Humphrey tells Clym that the lovers are meeting frequently. Finally, Thomasin takes matters into her own hands, telling Clym that a date for the wedding has been set.

---

**NOTE: The Footnote**    In a strange footnote, Hardy sketches for the reader his originally intended ending, where Thomasin remains widow and Diggory goes on in his isolated, weird life as a reddleman. The novelist suggests that the "true" ending is "the more consistent conclusion." Happy or unhappy—which ending is in fact the "more consistent" with the rest of the book? We know what Hardy believes, but all readers may not agree with him.

---

# CHAPTER 4: CHEERFULNESS AGAIN ASSERTS ITSELF AT BLOOMS-END, AND CLYM FINDS HIS VOCATION

On the morning of the wedding, the familiar crowd of villagers gathers at Fairway's cottage to make a goose-feather mattress for the newlyweds. As usual, Grandfer Cantle and Christian argue, and Fairway keeps the peace. The natures of the Egdon commonfolk do not change, as we know. Unexpectedly early, the wedding party passes by outside. This marriage has taken place rapidly, quite unlike Thomasin's first one. The villagers cheer the couple, an obviously popular pair.

That afternoon, Clym works alone upstairs on a sermon. He will not join the wedding feast in the evening, because he would not be happy in the company. Only two-and-a-half years earlier, it was unhappy Thomasin who would not participate in the Christmas party given for him. Hardy loves to remind us of these contrasts.

When the celebration begins at evening, Clym slips out unobserved and walks to a point where he can see Eustacia's former home. Charley, too, walks by, still depressed by Eustacia's death himself. He asks Clym for some keepsake that belonged to her. Back at Blooms-End, Clym gives the boy a lock of Eustacia's hair, which Charley kisses tearfully.

As the two go back out into the night, dim-sighted Clym asks Charley to describe what can be seen of the festivities through the window. The party is lively; no one misses Clym. Symbolically, perhaps, Clym has already begun his solitary life as a preacher, separated from the activities of ordinary people.

The following Sunday, Clym can be seen atop Rainbarrow, his wife's old lookout point. He is not waiting for romantic love, however; he is preaching about brotherly love to a group of heath men and women. This afternoon, his text is from the Bible, a reference to King Solomon's willingness to do his mother's will. Clym is still feeling guilty about his behavior toward his mother.

Hardy tells us that Clym will continue this new career, traveling widely. He will do well enough; some people will agree with his ideas, and everyone will be kind, because of what has happened to him.

---

**NOTE: Heroes or Villains?**     As the story ends, you may probably agree that no character has been really wicked. On the other hand, no character has been blameless. Although Hardy's characters are very different from each other, they do have this in common—like all human beings, they are a mixture of selfishness and generosity, of cruelty and kindness. And they are all affected by the arbitrary workings of fate.

---

# A STEP BEYOND

## Tests and Answers

### TESTS

## Test 1

1. A popular saying of the people of Egdon _____
   Heath was
   A. "The Quiet Woman is run by an unquiet
      man"
   B. "Eustacia Vye is the devil's own
      daughter"
   C. "No moon, no man"

2. Hardy solves the problem of exposition by _____
   A. letting us eavesdrop on the townsfolk
   B. writing short scenes in which Diggory
      Venn is featured
   C. flashbacks

3. Eustacia's signal to Damon Wildeve was _____
   A. the flowerpot in her window
   B. a bonfire
   C. the ship's flag over Captain Vye's roof

4. Thomas Hardy describes Eustacia as _____
      I. "the raw material of a divinity"
     II. possessed of "Pagan eyes, full of
         nocturnal mysteries"
    III. "heaven paying a visit to Earth"
   A. I and II only     B. II and III only
   C. I, II, and III

5. Eustacia confesses that her great desire is ____
   A. "to have a man destroy himself for her love"
   B. "to be loved to madness"
   C. "to have Wildeve beg to touch the hem of her gown"

6. Diggory Venn became a reddleman because ____
   A. he was too poor to have a farm
   B. Thomasin had rejected his marriage proposal
   C. he loved to breathe the air of Egdon Heath

7. Before Eustacia actually met Clym Yeobright, she dreamed about a man ____
   A. in silver armour
   B. on a white charger
   C. who tamed wild animals

8. When Thomasin finally married Wildeve, she was given away by ____
   A. Diggory Venn
   B. Eustacia Vye
   C. Clym Yeobright

9. Tradition is utilized by Hardy in the form of ____
      I. Guy Fawkes Day
     II. Christmas mumming
    III. Maypole festivities
   A. I and III only    B. II and III only
   C. I, II, and III

10. The background for Clym's proposal to Eustacia was ____
    A. the singing of the chorus
    B. an eclipse
    C. the sheep shearing ritual

11. Describe in detail the moral code that the people of Egdon Heath live by (or claim to). What behavior is considered decent, and what is considered unacceptable?

12. To what extent is Eustacia responsible for her tragic end, and to what extent is it influenced by the fate (or chance) that seems to operate so strongly in her life?

13. Explain in detail how Hardy uses images from nature to underscore, amplify, or anticipate the events of his story. Use at least five different examples.

14. Why are there so many references to ancient myth in the novel? Do these references give added dimension to the story, in your view, or do they distract from the action? How do they work, if in fact they do?

15. Diggory Venn is not a believable character, unless he is a supernatural being. Explain in full and use examples from the novel.

## Test 2

1. Mrs. Yeobright's trust, his plans to be a                  _____
   teacher, and Eustacia's happiness are
   problems which

   A. Clym must reconcile
   B. Clym's goals in life
   C. Clym's reasons for abandoning Paris

2. A major theme of this novel is                  _____
   A. the universe's indifference toward mankind
   B. the path of true love never does run smooth
   C. the best laid plans often go astray

3. Eustacia was hurt when          _____
   A. the 100 guineas were given to Thomasin
   B. she heard Clym singing as he cut furze
   C. she learned about the dice game by
      firelight

4. Mrs. Yeobright was denied admission to          _____
   Clym's house because
   A. Eustacia refused to see her
   B. of a misunderstanding
   C. it would have been embarrassing to
      Eustacia

5. Mrs. Yeobright characterized herself to          _____
   Johnny Nonsuch as
   A. "one who has seen the devil in
      petticoats"
   B. "a broken-hearted woman cast off by her
      son"
   C. "a devotee of anguish"

6. Thomasin's baby was named          _____
   A. Eustacia Clementine
   B. Rose of Sharon
   C. Heather Angel

7. Eustacia's young admirer, Charley,          _____
   A. arranged for her to leave the heath
   B. hid the pistols
   C. offered to defend her against Clym

8. The superstitious Susan Nonsuch          _____
   A. talked "in tongues" against Eustacia
   B. predicted the disaster after reading the
      tea leaves
   C. burned a wax effigy of Eustacia

9. The entire action of the novel takes place          _____
   A. within a year and a day
   B. between Clym's 26th and 29th birthdays
   C. in the course of two full years on Egdon
      Heath

10. The closing sentence of the novel contains          _____
    these words:
    A. "He was a romantic martyr to
       superstition"
    B. "But everywhere he was kindly received"
    C. "He might have been called the
       Rousseau of Egdon"

11. The world of this novel is neither entirely Christian nor
    entirely pagan. Discuss.

12. To many readers, the hero of the novel is Clym Yeo-
    bright. Giving at least three examples, discuss the ways
    in which Hardy focuses the book on him.

13. How is humor used in the novel? Choose at least three
    examples and explain their effect upon the action, the
    reader or the theme.

14. Hardy's use of coincidence is so artificial that his ideas
    about fate and free will cannot be taken seriously. Refer-
    ring to at least three incidents in the novel, discuss this
    topic.

15. Not excluding Eustacia, Hardy's women characters lack
    real depth. They are passive, conventional, and incapa-
    ble of growth. Agree or disagree, using examples from
    the text.

## ANSWERS

**Test 1**
1. C     2. A     3. B     4. A     5. B     6. B
7. A     8. B     9. C     10. B

**11.** Most of our knowledge of Egdon's prevailing moral code comes indirectly from the words, thoughts, and actions of those who care most about what other people think: Thomasin, of course, and Mrs. Yeobright. Go back and study what bothers them about Thomasin and Wildeve's first marriage attempt, for example, or look at Mrs. Yeobright's reaction to the rumors about Eustacia and Wildeve. But morality is not just a matter of appropriate conduct between men and women. What do the common people say about family responsibilities, about religion, about friendship? What do their actions show about communal loyalty? It might also be useful to look at the thoughts of those who seem to defy public morality. What, exactly, does Eustacia or Wildeve do that is inappropriate? And what does each refuse to do, because of a lingering belief in the morals of the day?

**12.** This question has no easy answer, and you may enjoy arguing both sides. In the eyes of many readers, Hardy himself wants to have it both ways. The way to approach this question is to look at Eustacia's crucial moments of decision, critical turning points in the action. What brings on tragedy—Eustacia's willfulness or an accidental turn of events? Is she forced to act in certain ways, or is she trapped by circumstances? Take several examples— her decision to marry Clym, her decision not to open the door for Mrs. Yeobright, her decision to leave with Wildeve, her decision to commit suicide in the end. In each case, discuss the relationship between Eustacia's will, her desire, and the actual options open to her. The question of any possible "guilt" is not the issue here, but "responsibility" is. You will want to re-read, too, what Eustacia herself felt about the issue.

**13.** Each reader will have his or her own favorite examples of Hardy's use of natural imagery. For variety, however, you will want to choose at least one that predicts the

course of events, as for example when the wind moans
through the trees at Devil's Bellows just before Mrs. Yeobright is turned out to her death. You will also want to write
about the use of nature to mirror a character's mood, as on
the dreary day when Clym leaves home to find a cottage for
Eustacia and himself. You will want to talk about natural
imagery used as symbol, as when the lush green ferns are
used to symbolize the fervent young love of Clym and
Eustacia. The most challenging and interesting natural symbol is, of course, the heath itself. It will be well worth the
effort to go back through the novel and decide for yourself
how this important symbol is used, how it changes, and
whether or not it is finally effective.

14.   If you enjoy mythology and ancient history, you
may readily understand Hardy's purposes in using so many
classical references. Looking particularly at his descriptions
of the heath or of Eustacia, you will see that his principal
technique is to make a parallel. What would we think of the
characters and events of the novel, if these ancient compar-
isons were not used? You do not, by the way, have to agree
that Hardy is always successful; you might decide that some
allusions work well, others do not. No matter what you
judge to be the case, be sure to explain why you have come
to your conclusions. Some readers feel that the classical references raise a simple country tale to the level of epic. You
may want to add your own opinion on this score.

15.   Concentrate on the unusual aspects of Venn's character and upon his unusual abilities, as demonstrated many
times in the story. Think of how the other characters react to
him, as when Eustacia cannot believe that anyone would
love as unselfishly as he seems to love Thomasin. What
about his magical capacity for turning up just in the nick of
time? Think how different the story would be if he did not
show up; in other words, does he act as a kind of agent for
good? If Diggory is supernatural, his powers are certainly

limited; you can point to many occasions when he cannot
change someone's mind. You will find much to talk about in
the nighttime gambling scene with Wildeve, however. Also,
consider Hardy's use of symbols associated with Diggory.
Finally, discuss how Hardy's original ending for the novel
affects your view of Diggory.

## Test 2

**1.** A  **2.** A  **3.** B  **4.** B  **5.** B  **6.** A

**7.** B  **8.** C  **9.** A  **10.** B

**11.**  When do the people of Egdon go to church, and
what happens when they do? Are their major celebrations
Christian, pagan, or a blend of the two? When strange and
terrible events occur, do these people tend to call on the
Christian God or do they fall back on ancient superstitious
beliefs? The answers to these questions are closely related to
this topic. Remember that Christianity can be interpreted
differently by different believers. You will also want to look
at the actions of the main characters, at their reactions to the
bad things that happen to them, and judge whether or not
they behave and think as Christians do. (Most of Hardy's
original readers, of course, would have thought of themselves as believing, practicing Christians, and that fact may
have affected his portrayal of Christian ideas.) Look at Clym
and his ministry. How does he resemble Christ, and how
does he differ? Does he decide to preach the 11th Com-
mandment because it is basic to Christian belief?

**12.**  To write this essay, you must decide what a hero is:
the most interesting character, the one who changes the
most, or the one who represents the author's ideas? Refer to
the major events of the book and show how they relate to
Clym and to his development as a human being. Explain
Clym's relationship with Hardy's important unifying symbol, the heath. Do you see a comparison between the

author's voice, which we hear clearly so often, and the thoughts of Clym? Think, too, of the end of the novel. It is Clym's life, alone, that seems to continue to grow and enlarge, leaving the reader behind. How does the sadness that has settled upon Clym mirror Hardy's own attitude toward the action of the novel? You may also want to discuss how Hardy puts the character he respects most to the severest tests.

**13.** Humor is very difficult to write about. Nonetheless, you will find that there is more than one kind of humor in this novel, and you can compare them. There is the lively joking of the country folk; there is the biting sarcasm used by major characters when they are under stress; and there are at least two kinds of humor directly from the author—his ironic comments to the reader, and his manipulation of the plot for grotesquely comic effects. Like Shakespeare, Hardy sometimes uses humor for "comic relief", to give our emotions a rest from the tension of tragedy. He also uses humor, which is an attention-getting device, to emphasize his themes.

**14.** Coincidence occurs frequently in the story, but you will want to choose only important moments. Probably the most important incident is when Mrs. Yeobright stands at the closed door at Clym's cottage, but there are the others—Clym's return just when Eustacia is considering Wildeve's proposal, the raffle which Christian wins at The Quiet Woman, Charley's lighting of Eustacia's bonfire. These incidents may be intended as examples of fate, but are they believable in terms of the story? You may want to explain how the chance occurrences of the plot are intended, in your view, to work upon the reader; for example, what happens to the reader's emotions when one of the coincidences is about to have an important effect upon the action? You may also want to define "fate" and "free will" in your own terms, so that your argument will be clearer.

**15.** For such a topic, as you discuss the women characters, compare them with the men; in other words, consider
also just how interesting and profound the *male* characters
are. Note that Clym, Wildeve, and Diggory have certain
advantages given them by society—education, an inheritance, and freedom of action, respectively. You will want to
explain both men and women in terms of the values of the
world in which they live. Why is Eustacia considered mannish? Why do we see Mrs. Yeobright almost entirely in her
role as mother? How does Thomasin change after marriage?
To discuss the women is to discuss their place in society, so
point out those occasions when their actions are hampered
by convention. You will also want to discuss the thoughts of
the women, so far as we know them. Are they limited by
lack of education or experience? And what about the
women's moral depth? You can find many examples of
decent motive and behavior which show a largeness of soul
in Thomasin, for instance, that even the idealistic Clym cannot really match.

# Term Paper Ideas

1.  Is Wildeve guilty of great wrongdoing, or is he the victim of fate? Using examples from the novel, explain how each interpretation is almost equally defensible.

2.  In what ways, and for what reasons, does Hardy distinguish Eustacia from the Egdon natives?

3.  How does a character's relationship to the bare surroundings and the simple village of Egdon Heath life reveal truths about the character?

4.  Compare Eustacia with Thomasin. Why would Damon and Clym be attracted to both of them?

5.  What are the good and the bad qualities of Damon? of Eustacia? of Diggory?

6.  Discuss the character of Christian. How is he used to place the other characters in perspective?

7.  What is the function of the scenes that involve *only* the rural bystanders? Show how they are important to the central story.

8.  To some, Egdon Heath is more than a dramatic setting; it is a major character in the novel. How does the heath play a role in the action? In what ways does it affect the human characters?

9.  Hardy portrays the Wessex countryside as ancient yet timeless. Why does he refer so frequently to prehistoric times? What is he saying, if anything, about the present and the future?

10.  How does Hardy use weather, seasonal changes, and natural objects to develop characters in this novel?

**11.** Many readers have viewed Hardy as a pessimistic writer, but he testily denied the label. What do you think is his philosophical point of view? Does he portray a just world?

**12.** What role does money play in the novel? Think of the effect it has upon, for example, Christian, Damon and Eustacia. How many unfortunate things happen because of lack of money? Does Hardy consider money itself an evil?

**13.** Almost every reference to marriage in the novel is ironic or bitter. Is Hardy criticizing the institution itself? Explain how marriage is an important theme in the narrative. Explore its importance in the society of Egdon Heath.

**14.** What does Hardy believe about passion as opposed to reason in human affairs? Does he think passion is always dangerous or wicked? What is his view of romantic love?

**15.** Is the novel completely "realistic," or can some events be explained only as the result of the influence of the supernatural? To what extent, for instance, does Hardy intend for us to believe the supernatural associations with Eustacia and Diggory?

# Further Reading
## CRITICAL WORKS

Butler, Lance St. John, ed. *Thomas Hardy After Fifty Years*. Totowa (NJ): Rowan and Littlefield, 1977. New interpretations of Hardy's fiction and poetry by well-known poets and academics.

Cox, R.G., ed. *Thomas Hardy, The Critical Heritage*. New York: Barnes & Noble, 1970. A large, important selection of reviews and critical comment written in Hardy's own time, 1871–1914.

Drabble, Margaret, ed. *The Genius of Thomas Hardy*. New York: Alfred Knopf, 1976. An illustrated collection of beautifully written essays by famous writers of today.

Guerard, Albert J., ed. *Hardy, A Collection of Critical Essays*. Englewood Cliffs: Prentice-Hall, 1963. An important collection of essays, including pieces by D.H. Lawrence and W.H. Auden.

Howe, Irving. *Thomas Hardy*. New York: Macmillan, 1968. A significant critical study focusing on Hardy's formative years and his philosophical skepticism.

Kramer, Dale, ed. *Critical Approaches to the Fiction of Thomas Hardy*. New York: Barnes & Noble, 1979. A wide variety of critical approaches in sophisticated essays by contemporary academics.

*Modern Fiction Studies*. Thomas Hardy issue, VI. Fall, 1960. An issue devoted entirely to the ideas and work of Thomas Hardy.

Page, Norman, ed. *Thomas Hardy, The Writer and his Background*. New York: St. Martin's, 1980. A collection of essays by contemporary scholars that explores Hardy's intellectual and historical background.

Smith, Anne, ed. *The Novels of Thomas Hardy*. New York: Barnes & Noble, 1979. Essays by scholars who have discovered new ways of reading and understanding Hardy's work.

*The Southern Review.* Thomas Hardy Centennial Issue, VI (Summer, 1940). Essays by poets and critics attesting to Hardy's influence on writing of the 20th century.

Sumner, Rosemary. *Thomas Hardy: Psychological Novelist.* New York: St. Martin's, 1981. An exploration of Hardy's understanding of unconscious drives, with a chapter on *"The Return of the Native*—the psychological problems of modern man and woman."

# AUTHOR'S OTHER WORKS
## (a selection)

*Under the Greenwood Tree*, 1872. A gentle, humorous tale of a village love affair that, after many misunderstandings, ends happily.

*Far From the Madding Crowd*, 1874. A realistic story about how one woman finally finds her true love after a bad marriage.

*The Mayor of Casterbridge*, 1886. The tale of how a poor but ambitious man rises to great heights only to be destroyed by flaws in his character.

*The Woodlanders*, 1887. A neglected novel about an ill-starred romantic triangle, strangely mixing happiness and tragedy.

*Wessex Tales*, 1888. A collection of short stories using Wessex legends and folk traditions.

*Tess of the D'Urbervilles*, 1891. The popular classic about a young girl driven to murder when her life is ruined by forces beyond her control.

*Jude the Obscure*, 1896. A gloomy, brooding story of a young man and his unconventional love life, ending in failure and early death.

*Selected Shorter Poems of Thomas Hardy.* John Wain, ed. St. Martin's Press, New York, 1966. A few of Hardy's short poems, including selections from *Wessex Poems* and *Poems of the Past and Present.*

# Glossary

**"Barley Mow"**   A famous and racy country song

**Bustard**   A big, long-legged game bird

**Courser**   A particularly lively and graceful horse

**Dab**   An expert

**Domesday**   *Domesday Book*, an ancient British record of land values and ownership compiled in 1086

**Furze**   A dark evergreen shrub found on wastelands

**Gallicrow**   A scarecrow

**Galloway**   A small, very hardy horse

**Heath**   A large open area of wasteland; a moor

**Knap**   The top of a hill

**Lammas-tide**   The 1st of August (Lammas Day), traditional celebration of the first harvest

**Michaelmas**   The 29th of September, feast day of St. Michael and the beginning of autumn

**Mummers**   Masked actors in Christmas pantomimes

**Ogee**   A curve shaped like an *S*

***Pis aller***   The last resort

**Pitt Diamond**   Crown jewel of the last kings of France

**Rames**   A skeleton

**Reddle** (*Redding*)   An orange-red dye used on sheep

**Serpent**   An old-fashioned snake-shaped wind instrument, sounding like a modern bassoon

**Skimmity-ride**   A boisterous rural procession staged to make fun of a spouse who has been unfaithful or has been betrayed

**Slack-twisted**   Lethargic, inactive

**Stave**   A song

**Tussaud collection**   Madame Tussaud's, a world-famous London wax museum

**Vicinal way**   A small local road

**Vlankers**   Sparks

**Zany**   A simpleton or fool

# The Critics

Eustacia Vye despises the heath and the workfolk . . . [she] embodies the decadence of the bourgeoisie, who, for want of anything better, glorify the individual.
—G.W. Sherman, *The Pessimism of Thomas Hardy*, 1976

. . . in spite of the fact that the agonies endured by Hardy's characters are not arbitrarily inflicted by the gods or Fate or the President of the Immortals, but organically derive from their being *the kind of people they are*, still, Hardy intimates, there is immense sorrow in the fact that things are as they are . . . . Life *is* painful, existence *is* an agony to be endured—to deny that Hardy felt this is to misread him, perversely or wrong-headedly.
—Geoffrey Thurley, *The Psychology of Hardy's Novels*, 1975

He wrote and wrote again, and he never found it easy. He lacked elegance, he never learned the trick of the whip-lash phrase, the complicated lariat twirling of the professed stylists . . . .
—Katherine Anne Porter, *Notes on a Criticism of Thomas Hardy*, 1940

In both his novels and his poetry Hardy's thoughts revolve frequently around the comic or tragic irony of the mischances of the marital relation . . . . At the root of his polemics are his sense of the injustice of imposing a permanent bond as the penalty for a passing desire and his knowledge of the numberless instances in which love has been stifled by obligation.
—Samuel Chew, *Thomas Hardy, Poet and Novelist*, 1929

It is the force of circumstance—the malignant power of Egdon Heath to dwarf and thwart the aspiring soul—that drives Eustacia Vye to irretrievable disaster.

It is circumstance too that involves her husband in the same calamity, for he can hardly be held more fortunate in escaping with his life. His mother falls beneath a stroke of fortune utterly undeserved.

—J.W. Cunliffe, *English Literature During the Last Half-Century*, 1923

[Hardy's] creative power shows itself most continuously and most characteristically in its capacity to embody its inspiration in visible form. Before he does anything else, Hardy wants to make you see with your mind's eye the action of the tale he is telling. Indeed, his creative impulse seems to have instinctively expressed itself in picture.

—David Cecil, *Hardy the Novelist*, 1946